Montana's Rivers
of Liquid Ice

*A collection of poetry from Montana's
award-winning "Cowboy Poet"*

James H. Kinsey

This book is dedicated to Nancy,
my wife of 52 years, who has
worked tirelessly to make sure
this book came to fruition.

Thanks to my brother-in-law,
John Carnes who worked to put
everything together for publishing.

Cover photograph of Rocky Mountain Front
near Augusta, Montana (on private land)
By James Michael Kinsey © 2019
Cinematographer and Executive Producer of
Skull Bound TV
www.SkullBoundTV.com

Cover design © 2019
Steve Parisi

CONTENTS

INTRODUCTION

The seed for this book started to grow back in August of 1985 when I moved my family out to the wilds of Montana.

We had sold our little farm in Thurmont, Maryland, to answer God's call in helping children in need, and while doing that, Montana grabbed not only my heart, but also my soul. In fact, it was seven years before I was to write my very first poem called "Montana In Time," which was to win the Diamond Homer Award in a nation-wide contest. That poem has been followed by hundreds of other poems over the years and there seemed to be no end in sight.

This land of Montana is like no other place found on our planet Earth, and now it is the only place where the fresh footsteps of resting angels lie. It's where the best of God can be found no matter where one might look. It's a foretaste of what Heaven is all about.

Montana is about the people: The Native Americans and the Cowboys who carved their own human dreams long ago out of the wildness; the people of today who are the guardians of those to come and their coming tomorrows; the animals and the mighty mountains; and the endless western soul-changing blue sky. It's about our own journey and the needed search for food for our soul that makes us each the person we are.

I hope you enjoy it.

James Hilton Kinsey
Cowboy.Poet@outlook.com

STRAIGHT FROM MY HEART

Straight from my heart
from me to you
I offer my thoughts about Montana
in its cowboy colors of sagebrush purple and big-sky blue;

My thoughts of this western Eden in which I live;
My thoughts of the many truths of its beauty to you I give;
My thoughts of the endless gifts and what they really mean;
My thoughts of the rainbows and sunsets in which I dream;

My thoughts for our souls; for here they'll richly feed;
My thoughts about the wild flowers born from Heaven's seeds;
My thoughts of the mighty waters running cold and western-pure;
My thoughts of why this land, one's heart can rebuild and cure;

So, straight from my heart
from me to you
I offer my thoughts about Montana in which I live
in its cowboy colors of sagebrush purple and big-sky blue.

MY LIVING SIGN

Before I die, I've sought to leave
something of myself behind
for the coming generations from my seed.
These poems I've left for you as My Living Sign.

A sign that I was really here.
My life's journey I truly did enjoy
for I've learned that love is God's greatest gift
given to each of us to cherish and honor, not destroy.

So, before I die, I've sought to leave
something of myself behind
for the coming generations from my seed
these poems I've left for you as My Living Sign.

RIVERS OF LIQUID ICE

Eagle screams and lazy summer dreams
and wild trout swimming in Rivers Of Liquid Ice
Sky busting mountains, vast wind-swept plains
This place called Montana, one's soul does tease and entice

Chilling sounds from a bugling bull elk
on a cold, first mating, fall's early light
More stars than one's heart could ever count
nightly shining down here, each so clear and remembered bright

Ancient thunder of millions of slaughtered buffalo
Their ghost spirits this land still feels and knows
Deep powder from a winter's arctic storm
A skier's rush, descending in its fresh virgin snows

Towering pines and endless sunsets of every color known
mixed-in with the voices of wolves running wild and free
Western skies of unmatched crystal glory
A circle of stones found from a long vanished Indian tepee

For it will tempt you with eagle screams and lazy summer dreams
and wild trout swimming in Rivers Of Liquid Ice
There are busting mountains, vast wind-swept plains
This place called Montana, one's soul does daily tease and entice

PARADISE FOUND

In Paradise Found where eagles fly
and snowy mountains touch crystal skies,
my heart has found the peace it needs
and that taste of Heaven, my soul to feed.

Its history is rich and has much to tell
of Indians and settlers and Custer who fell.
Their bones are now scattered far and wide.
Its mighty rivers still carry each tear they cried.

Now nowhere else on this earth my friend
since it's only here where a broken-spirit this land can mend.
You see this place is not really hard to find.
Just look westward and you'll see Montana's paradise sign.

For within its vast lands where eagles still fly
and snowy mountains touch crystal skies,
one can still find the peace one needs
and that taste of Heaven, one's soul to feed.

LIVIN' IN THIS COWBOY LAND

Spurs and ropes and wild horses that run
Livin' In This Cowboy Land is hard work, but so much fun.
We've got the endless western skies to ride below,
and we'll race every tumble weed that the west wind blows.

Our summers are dead-dry; our winters long and bitter cold.
Our hearts are horse-crazy and our souls are fearless bold.
Our faces are well weathered from the wind and the sun.
We'll even rope a cloud's shadow just to have some midday fun.

Our horses are fast, they're our very best friends.
They help us herd the cattle and busted fences mend.
We live a simple life, we even talk to God.
We make our livin' with a red-hot branding rod.

Our guns are Colts and Winchesters of blue steel.
We hang every cattle thief who our cattle steal.
Our nights are spent with the stars far above our heads
as we dream of our straw mattresses on our wooden bunkhouse beds.

For we love our spurs, our ropes and the wild horses that run
Livin' In This Cowboy Land is hard work, but so much fun.
We've the endless western skies to ride below,
and we'll race every tumble weed that the west wind blows.

THESE WINDS OF MONTANA

They're born of her mountainous breath
These Winds Of Montana that we know.
They cause our towering pines to whisper and roar
and sweep in our deep winters of stinging, lasting snow.

They give our pure air a crystal-like feel
and always sweep our stormy skies to a remembered blue.
They'll send our western tumbleweeds on a racing blur
and sometimes keep them racing the whole day through.

They howl on our fall nights when the moon is asleep
and bring the needed rains that quench our deep western thirst.
They'll sometimes whisper things to our sleeping human hearts
then loudly awaken us to another new day's rising sunburst.

They can carry a kite straight toward Heaven's distant door
and can stop its flight in the twinkling of an eye.
Then start all over again before we have a second thought
and send it racing upward, back into our Montana clear sky

For they're born of her mountainous breath
These Winds Of Montana that we know.
They cause our towering pines to whisper and roar
and sweep in our deep winters of stinging, lasting snow.

THE RODEO RIDER

The Rodeo Rider:
now he's hard-lean, ranch-grown, and western tough.
A living type of hard-working cowboy
who plays the rodeo game, riding crazy and cowboy rough.

He's earned every one of his riding scars
and spends his rodeo nights in small town dancing bars.
He walks western-proud but a little bronco-bent
and drives a dusty old pickup and pays no-man, no address rent.

He's at his highest, his cowboy best,
when atop a wild critter, riding to beat its eight-second test,
and if he finishes the rodeo without breaking any bones,
he's praying his winnings will pay off a few overdue loans.

Now he dreams mostly of owning a sweet-water ranch
with a little house in the cooling shade of a cottonwood branch;
to have a loving wife who'll share her all and give
maybe a few kids to raise and in the west, forever live.

For he loves the western lands in which he was born,
to uphold its deep values within his heart, he's sworn;
for he's one of the toughest cowboys you'll ever meet or see.
He's born of lightning and thunder; born to be wild and free.

ON THE EVENING'S COOLING WIND
(A MONTANA COWBOY'S PRAYER)

Please forgive this old Montana cowboy, Lord,
from my many cowboy sins.
Please guide me, Lord,
for it's Your ranch I seek to someday win.

Please save me, Lord,
keep me safe from all the temptations I daily see.
Please hear me, Lord,
and answer my heart's calling plea.

Please teach me, Lord,
to cast my barroom dreams away.
Please help me, Lord,
to no longer from Your wisdom stray.

Please hold me real close, Lord, and let me not fall ever again.
Please, let me once again, Lord,
start to hear Your voice,
On The Evening's Cooling Wind.

So please forgive this old Montana cowboy, Lord.
Forgive me of my many cowboy sins.
Please guide me, Lord, for it's Your ranch
this old Montana cowboy seeks to win.

CITY MAN'S DECAY

Now the Montana cowboy's soul is truly different.
It's hard, western-weathered and always cattle bound;
loves the great life he daily lives
and understands Montana's every living, breathing sound.

Their souls talk to God every given night
when the western stars speak of his glory.
They carry deep within their hearts
every known, past told, Montana cowboy story.

Their love for Montana's great vastness
is deep and everlasting and honor-true;
For every Montana cowboy's favorite color is
pure, big-sky, every day, endless rodeo blue.

Every one of their souls was made for riding horses
from the early dawn to a sunset's fading day;
each loves the heavy smell of dusty cattle
and holding down every brawling, to-be-branded, wild stray.

They well understand Montana's uniqueness
and of the many treasures of its given remembered way;
for each Montana cowboy's soul is truly western pure
and plain empty of the disease called, City Man's Decay.

So, you see, the Montana cowboy's soul, is really different.
It's hard western-weathered and always cattle bound;
for it loves the great life it daily lives
and truly understands Montana's every living, breathing sound.

THIS LAND MONTANA

This land Montana, a place of dream seekers and cloud watchers;
a land filled with vastness and endless Winchester colored skies;
a place of found Indian spirit-visions and the felt freshness
of everyone who once lived within her first wildness, then died.

Her depth of her beauty is beyond the reach of the city heart.
Her mountains bear the full weight of God's many gifts seen.
Her streams still hold all of her first children's many tears.
Her fertile skies the first place to hear an eagle scream.

She's a gift, a foretaste of Heaven, to each hungry human soul
once accepted, you'll never be the same again;
for she's a living, breathing, treasure to all those
whose hearts have learned to listen to her singing wild winds.

Wild winds that sing of her dream seekers, her cloud watchers;
songs of her vastness, her endless Winchester colored skies;
songs of her found Indian spirit-visions and the felt freshness
of everyone who once lived within her first wildness, then died.

THE SHADOW LANDS

In The Shadow Lands below Montana's snowy mountains,
in that special place of echoing elk screams,
there still live wild horses and thundering buffalo
and real working cowboys, it so seems.

There are pure running rivers and ancient living trees;
dancing Indian spirits and icy crystal streams;
a place to renew our tired human souls,
fulfiller of many of our sometimes, wishing dreams.

There's a boldness of standing beauty to find,
and the crafty high-mountain mule deer.
A paradise of wilderness to daily discover
where the doorway of Heaven, in its sunsets, daily appear.

It's a summer Eden of humming birds of tiny fierceness
and howling wolves and the mighty grizzly bear.
A land of deep and everlasting uniqueness
that's now so hard to find and now so earthly rare.

It births forth the painter and the poet;
Their given gifts born of its shared, whispered dreams;
for each sees deeply within its western soul
and then paint and speak of its vast treasured scenes;

For in The Shadow Lands below Montana's snowy mountains,
in that special place of echoing elk screams,
there still live wild horses and thundering buffalo
and real working cowboys, it so seems.

CRYSTAL COWBOY BLUE

To wander, to ride wild and endlessly free
has always been my heart's longing and deepest plea.
To own a fine horse, to shoot straight and true
To live beneath God's western skies of Crystal Cowboy Blue

To own a large herd of longhorn beef
To live a life without tears or the pain of grief
To find that very special western gal
To have her share my life as wife, lover, and best-friend pal

To drink from cold pure mountain streams
To raise lots of children and share their dreams
To watch each winter's snow fall, white and soft
To listen to a summer's rain from a dry hayloft

To own a great ranch as far as the eye can see
To listen to the windy whispers of ancient pine trees
To ride where no one has ever ridden before
To have a cowboy's heart for all who stop at my front door

So, to wander, to ride wild and endlessly free
will always be my heart's longing and deepest plea.
To own a fine horse, to shoot straight and true
To live beneath God's western skies of Crystal Cowboy Blue

SALT AND PEPPER

I've felt the wildness of a new day's dawn
as it streaked across a wide Montana summer sky.
I've heard the calling sounds
from a long-tailed, flying magpie.

I've seen over its wind-still waters
an eagle's shadow scream.
I've seen her native trout swimming
within her cold flowing streams.

I've seen her snowy mountains shine
under a full moon's winter's light.
I've talked to the stars of her heavens
as they looked down on my own soul, each diamond-bright.

I've seen the richness of her western vastness
where the deer and antelope freely roam.
I've seen the true strength of her brave people
and the great pride they have in calling Montana their home.

I've seen their many hardships
and their wealth of Heaven's given grace.
I've seen their broad western smiles
and their lands buried deep in white snowy lace.

I've watched them survive their bitter, long winters
and listened to their remembered dreams of spring.
I've seen them pray for an early thaw
and watched their river frogs of summer sing.

I've come to love and admire them all
and the great western land in which they've taken root,
for they are the Salt and Pepper of our American west.
They ride fast horses, wear guns, cowboy hats, and boots.

For I've felt the wildness of a new day's dawn
as it streaked across one of their wide, Montana summer skies.
I've heard the calling sounds
from one of their long-tailed, flying magpies.

PURE WESTERN DELIGHT

This Bitterroot Valley, it feeds the soul
within its season of summer and season of winter white.
Its high mountains reach down and touch each human heart
and fills them with their warmth of Pure Western Delight.

This valley is known for its summer green and stillness
found within the early mornings of its every awakening day.
Its silent river flows endlessly toward a distant salted sea
where the forgotten memories of many lost sailors lay.

Its gentle breath is heard within its soft-whispered wind
that falls from Heaven's distant door.
It welcomes all who travel to its gentle land
whether they're old or young, rich man or beggar poor.

For this Bitterroot Valley is God's special gift
where one can taste a little of Heaven's perfect peace.
Its vast and deep beauty is of God's very best
and far from the growing decay of our distant American east.

For this Bitterroot Valley, it daily feeds the soul
within its season of summer and season of winter white.
Its high mountains reach down and touch each human heart
and fills them with their warmth of Pure Western Delight.

WHERE THE HEART OF HEAVEN LAYS

Come to my land the west winds cry.
Come to where my sleeping buffalo lie.
Come and see my rugged mountains high.
Come and breathe in my pure blue sky.

Come and receive the gift of my western ways.
Come and walk Where the Heart of Heaven Lays.
Come and trust, fear not my winds calling voice.
Come and taste, let your tired soul then rejoice.

Come quickly now, don't say no.
Come to drink the coolness of my white melted snow.
Come now, don't waste yet another day.
Come my western dreamer, hear what I say.

Come and feel my rainbows on a rainy summer's day.
Come and receive the gift of my western way.
Come to a life far richer than any other kind.
Come, it's the best life within me you'll find.

So, come quickly, no longer delay.
Come to where my sleeping buffalo lay.
Come and receive the gift of my western ways.
Come and walk Where the Heart of Heaven Lays.

PREACHER MAN

Preacher Man is what many called him.
To others he was known as "the angel of death."
When anger removed his preacher's white collar
many a foolish cowboy took his very last, sinner's breath.

Now he rode throughout early Montana
taking the gospel to every one of its lawless towns,
riding in with his worn Bible and packing a gun.
He was always heard singing Heaven's hallelujah sound.

There was no man born to be any faster.
He could preach or draw his gun at the speed of light.
As God was always there standing right beside him
to give this Preacher Man his gun-slinging might.

Some say he died old in his sleep.
Some say he was near a hundred and ten.
But others I know say he's still riding the Montana lands.
Still seeking the lost to save, enlighten, and defend.

For the Preacher Man is what many called him.
To others he was known as "the angel of death."
When anger removed his preacher's white collar
many a foolish cowboy took his very last, sinner's breath.

THE UNKNOWN COWBOY

Now, the unknown cowboy's grave marker
still bears his long-ago dying date.
Third grave on the left, my friend,
once you pass Boot Hill's old rusty gate.

He was known to have been really fast.
He was known to have been really good,
but I guess he really wasn't, you see
for he was twenty when they buried him, in a coffin of wood.

History knows not his real given name.
It's said no one really ever knew
but he's still remembered to this very day
for his youthful eyes of wild gunfighter-blue.

They say a faded picture of an older woman was later found.
His dear mother some thought it could be.
What a long-ago shame for her back then
to never again his blue gunfighter eyes to see.

For he was shot through the heart one stormy August night.
It was a 44-40 that ended this short and foolish life.
He died hard in a gambling house; it was his twentieth birthday.
They say he was fighting over someone's young, wayward wife.

So now he lies beneath the unknown cowboy's grave marker.
It still bears his long-ago dying date.
Third grave on the left, my friend,
once you pass Boot Hill's old rusty gate.

WHERE ALL RAINBOWS ARE BORN

Now, it's here in Montana, Where All Rainbows Are Born
that travel across all our earth each evening and morn.'
Every color is painted by God's creative hands.
All rainbows seen traveling across all our earth's given lands.

They are sent to wash away our sometimes sadness and pain
when their colors they display, in a dark storm's falling rain,
to speak to our longing and drifting human hearts
saying "look to Heaven to be saved and smart."

They carry in their colors, God's very own promise
never to flood our earth again.
They each sing of His endless and loving glory
that lies far above our earth and its ever-deepening sins.

They bring us joy, just when we seem to need it the most
as they travel across all our living lands.
They speak of God's promised, new coming earth
all rainbows formed by His creation hand.

For it's only in Montana Where All Rainbows Are Born
that travel across our earth, each evening and morn'
Every color is painted by God's creative hands
all rainbows seen traveling across all our earth's given lands.

A VERY SPECIAL PLACE

This place called Montana is far more than seen treasure.
It's far more than anyone's soul could ever use.
It's more than endless pure-tasted joy,
for it's A Very Special Place, to be lived and never abused.

It's a land of all of God's very given best
where the loving touch of His hand is everywhere seen
from its eastern rolling, dry and windy vastness
to its mighty western mountains, that toward Heaven still lean.

Its big sky still runs the daily color, of angel painted blue.
Its many waters still flow icy cold, fresh and clean.
Its emerald green valleys still richly contain
the first echoing sounds of Eden's wild eagle screams.

It's where God still comes to walk in the evening cool
and where His trout still swim in waters of melted snowy lace.
You'll hear His breath in the winds that cross its lands,
for this place called Montana, is full of His created grace,

For it's far, more than seen treasure.
It's far more than anyone's soul could ever use.
It's far more than endless pure-tasted joy,
for it's A Very Special Place to be lived and never abused.

NEW SADDLES

Now old cowboys never die,
or cheat at cards or ever lie.
They just ride out to seek new trails
to look for new adventures so they can spin taller tales,

For it's among our stars where they nightly ride,
every cowboy that ever branded a wild cow's fly-infested hide,
and on New Saddles of Heaven's silver and gold
they ride forever young; they ride forever bold.

Now sometimes they've been seen lassoing a flying angel
and sometimes they've been known to ride a fiery comet too.
They're forever leaving behind their personal brand
on each bright star as they nightly ride our heavens through,

So, you see old cowboys, well, they never die,
or cheat at cards or ever lie.
They just ride out to seek new trails
to look for new adventures so they can spin taller tales.

BEST BUDDIES

It was a Red Ryder
and it was my very first BB gun.
It gave me my early years
of childhood, first-shootin' fun.

It brought me many endless smiles
to my then, and long-ago, youthful face
when I shot up zillions of empty soda bottles
at a terrific, little cowboy, shootin' pace.

Now many a neighbor cats' rear end
felt its surprising, smacking sting,
for I kept them out of my mother's flower beds.
I always kept them from doing their natural thing.

Now, even after all these many passing years
I can still remember the shootin' fun I once had.
I only wish I had kept my first BB gun
given to me, on a long-ago Christmas, by my lovin' Dad.

For it was a Red Rider
and it was my very first BB gun.
It was to fill me with endless happy memories
of my Dad and me havin' Best Buddies, shootin' fun.

JUST EVERYTHING WESTERN

Now, what makes a cowboy the way he is?
Is it where he's born or the way his heart seeks to live?
Was he touched special by God's own branded hands,
or is it that his soul can only feed in the western lands?

Maybe it's the call of its endless blue, eagle-filled skies
or is it the unique smell of sagebrush and coyote cries?
Is it the special feel of saddle leather, spurs and cowboy boots,
or is it their personal distaste for the look of big city suits?

Maybe it's their desire to sleep under the diamond-like stars,
or is it their need to carry a few hard-earned, rodeo scars?
Is it their unfillable hunger for a fast horse to daily ride,
or is it their quest for profound stillness that only the west provides?

Maybe it's their deep need to pack a loaded, silver six-gun,
or is it to rope and brand cattle in the hot western sun?
Is it their desire to eat each evening's meal from an open fire,
or is it Just Everything Western to quench their own burning human desires?

So just what makes a cowboy the way he is?
Is it where he's born or the way his heart seeks to live?
Was he touched special by God's own branded hands,
or is it Just Everything Western found only in the west's, Rocky Mountain lands?

COWBOY LAND

Just where lies this place called Cowboy Land?
Is it found only where tall cactus grow in bone-dry sand?
Is it really a place of circling buzzards and searing heat;
drinking saloons and card sharks who always five-ace cheat?

Or could there be far more to it than meets the eye?
Could there be within it lush green valleys and soft blue skies?
Might one find great rivers flowing and good cattle grass,
that place where our hearts will find true peace at last?

So just where lies this place called Cowboy Land?
Is it found only where tall cactus grow in bone-dry sand?
Is it really a place of circling buzzards and searing heat;
drinking saloons and card sharks who always five-ace cheat?

A COWBOY'S CUP OF TIN

Barbed wire and nesting blue birds
and the screaming sounds of a high mountain's savage wind.
A summer storm rainbow and prancing mule deer
and steaming black coffee in A Cowboy's Cup of Tin.

Wooden wagon wheels and found arrow heads
and long forgotten shallow pioneer graves
Many shattered dreams and found wealth
after the freeing of the Civil War slaves.

Texas longhorns and the first great cattle drives
and the plain's buffalo that the railroad sent forever away
A vast land raped and stolen from its first born
by hordes of white men full of greed and decay.

Deadly six-guns and famous outlaws
when the west was wild, young and free
The remembered names of Tombstone and Dodge City
and hanging ropes swinging from their busy, hanging tree.

Stagecoaches, dancing bar girls
and endless lonely nights spent with a spooky cattle herd
The awakening smells coming from the chuck wagon
and its sounds of frying slab bacon, smoked and cured.

One room schools and white wooden churches
and mining towns that sprung up overnight
A land in great turmoil and fast change
that stunned its first masters watching the sight.

For my heart sees its barbed wire and nesting blue birds
and hears the screaming sounds of a high mountain's savage wind.
It sees its summer storm rainbows and prancing mule deer
as I drink steaming black coffee in A Cowboy's Cup of Tin.

A COWBOY'S LIFE WAS

A Cowboy's Life Was broken fingers on callused hands,
healing rope burns earned working the cow producing lands.
Many days of hardship, some days of virgin peace,
most were spent herding cattle for the ever-hungry east.

His early days were full of danger
all lived riding beneath the west's blazing hot sun.
Days of great uncertainty, each with the fear of death,
so, all days were lived to the fullest from breath to breath.

Days of mending fences, days of snow and horse-killing cold.
His endless days of hard work that turned young men old.
Days of hard loneliness, days of joy and pain,
those lasting days of dryness, always praying for rain.

So, A Cowboy's Life Was broken fingers on callused hands,
ever healing rope burns earned working the cow producing lands.
Many days of hardship, some days of virgin peace,
for most were spent herding cattle for the ever-hungry east.

SADDLES

I've seen saddles in silver and saddles in gold.
I've seen saddles built for cowboys both brave and bold.
I've seen saddles for herding and saddles for following the sun.
I've seen saddles built plain for old-fashioned riding fun.

I've seen saddles that were new and saddles that were old.
I've seen saddles used in summer and winter's snowy cold.
I've seen saddles for gun fighters and saddles for the common man,
for it was the saddle that helped tame our Montana land.

So, I've seen saddles in silver and saddles in gold
I've seen saddles built for cowboys both brave and bold.
I've seen saddles for herding and saddles for following the sun,
but most saddles I've seen were built plain for old fashioned riding fun.

THE MOUNTAINS OF THUNDER

There's a mystical place called The Mountains Of Thunder
where the Indians still live white-man free;
a place where they still ride shoeless wild horses
and enjoy any buffalo they see.

They still live as they've lived since the beginning of time,
protected from the many sins of the white man's way.
They live fearlessly below The Mountains of Thunder
whose dream shadows hide all their given land every day.

Their tepees stand in uncountable numbers
reaching as far as the eagle can fly.
They live in eternal peace and natural harmony
beneath the Great Spirit's endless western sky.

For there's a mystical place called The Mountains Of Thunder
where the Indians still live white-man free;
a place where they still ride shoeless wild horses
and enjoy any buffalo they see.

THE MONTANA COWBOY

Now The Montana Cowboy has a rich life to live.
It has true meaning and has so much to offer and give.
He's got God's western skies to daily live below
and cattle drives to work in the light of a summer's moonglow.

He lives below great mountain ranges covered with winter's breath
and has clean rivers far from mankind's dirty cities of death.
He enjoys a daily freshness of air, still pure and angel clean
and is far away from the lands of big business and their machines.

He shares a oneness with God here, no other way found
and knows the fullness he has for working Montana's ground.
He has peace in his soul and daily food for his heart
and knows that livin' his way is more than just smart.

For every Montana cowboy has a rich life to live.
It has true meaning for them and has so much to offer and give.
For they've got God's western skies to daily live below
and cattle drives to work in the light of a summer's moonglow.

THE COWBOY WESTERN WAY

Now some say a cowboy's heart is different;
that it's as big as their western blue sky;
that it's far kinder and more understanding
and always able to comfort most anyone's cry.

Some say they're much closer to God
because they live within His creation every day;
that they have a richer and deeper grasp
of what it means to live The Cowboy Western Way.

Now others say they couldn't live that way
because their western winters are long and bitter cold.
But what do those folks really know about cowboy livin'
and about being tough, brave and western-bold.

For the cowboy's heart is a bigger heart,
it's as big as their western blue sky.
It's far more kind and understanding
and always ready to comfort most anyone's cry.

BRANDED

Branded is the heart
that's ever dreamed of living the cowboy's way.
Branded is the soul
that's ever worked a cowboy's hard-working day.

Branded are the eyes
that have ever watched a western setting sun.
Branded is the hand
that's held a blazing six-gun.

Branded is the breath
that's ever mixed with sage brush and pine-scented air.
Branded is everyone
who's ever watched a rodeo at a summer-ending fair.

Branded is every thought
that comes from a branded mind.
Branded are their tomorrows,
for all who carry a cowboy's branded sign.

For Branded is the human heart
that's dreamed of living the cowboy's way.
Branded is each human soul
that's ever worked a cowboy's hard-working day.

HEAVEN'S OWN

Now every time a real working cowboy has been born,
he's been made from the strongest of all western stock.
His cattleman's backbone has always been hand-carved,
carved from Heaven's Own, rocky mountain rock.

He's always been rugged and far-away different
from the modern make-up of the city livin' man
whose great difference has been so easily seen
in the inner softness of a pair of city-workin' hands.

For the real cattle-working western cowboy
he's never fancied much toward wearing city suits or ties.
He's always been a hard-working type of honest outdoor man
who never had to live by the art of telling, slick, city-man salesman lies.

You see, he's always been far more at home in a leather saddle
than any other kind of lifestyle found.
His soul has always been full of the west's high mountain winds,
and plum empty of the numbing madness of city machine sounds.

He's always been blessed with a heart full of true grit,
and a deep passion for good old common western cowboy sense.
He always carried a gun because it's his God-given birth-right,
and has used it only for his own human or family's self-defense.

So you see, every time a real working cowboy is born,
he's always made of the strongest of all western stock.
For his cattleman's backbone is always hand carved,
carved from Heaven's Own, rocky mountain rock.

BUFFALO LAND

In Buffalo Land of long ago,
all the grasses grew tall and green
and every tepee stood proud back then
in family villages by pure water streams.

In Buffalo Land of long-ago,
before the devouring shadow of the white man came
its endless prairie lands were peaceful and full
of bountiful, free roaming, wild game.

In Buffalo Land of long-ago,
all waters then flowed fresh and pure.
Its native peoples
had long learned its harshness to endure.

In Buffalo Land of long-ago,
the sound of gunfire was never heard,
or the betraying voice
of the coming white man's worthless word.

In Buffalo Land of long-ago,
its vastness was empty of the logger's cry.
It knew not the hurt of airplane engines
racing through its then peaceful, virgin sky.

In Buffalo Land of long ago,
the night light came from a fire's glow and distant stars.
There was no foul smell back then
from dirty, gasoline-eating, polluting cars

In Buffalo Land of long-ago,
the spoken story filled each child's nightly dreams.
Not one mind was ever ruined back then
by the curse of color TV screens.

In Buffalo Land of long-ago,
each life was lived day by day.
There were no such things as bad films
to destroy one's soul like today's filth and decay.

In Buffalo Land of long-ago,
its people lived in a time of endless, breathable room.
There were no great cities full of lost souls then,
with heavy hearts cast of modern concrete and gloom.

In Buffalo Land of long-ago,
every meal was cooked on an open fire.
There were no fancy modern kitchens then
or fancy cooks for one to hire.

For it was in Buffalo Land of long-ago,
when all the grasses grew tall and green
and every tepee stood proud
in family villages by pure water streams.

MOUNTAIN MADNESS

It's well known here in the west
that once someone drinks from a cold Montana mountain stream
they'll lose their heart to her,
for her Mountain Madness will enter their every nightly dream.

They'll dream of her deep beauty
and of her endless eagle-filled skies.
They'll dream of her racing plains antelope
and her great forests that below her mountain winds lie.

They'll dream of her western richness,
for she alone bears the hand of Heaven true.
They'll drift upon her mighty rivers
and wash their soul in her trout streams of crystal blue.

And when they taste the soft wetness
off one of her wild flowers, in morning dew.
They'll never be same ever again
no matter what they try to say or do.

So, take heed to these words, my friend.
Should you ever drink from a high mountain, Montana stream
you're sure to lose your heart to her,
for Mountain Madness will enter your every nightly dream.

THE COWBOY WESTERN WAY

Now some say a cowboy's heart is different,
that it's as big as their western blue sky;
that it's far kinder and more understanding
and always able to comfort most anyone's cry.

Some say they're much closer to God
because they live within His creation every day;
that they have a richer and deeper grasp
of what it means to live The Cowboy Western Way.

Now others say they couldn't live that way
because their western winters are long and bitter cold,
but what do those folks really know about cowboy livin'
and being tough, brave and western-bold.

For the cowboy's heart is a bigger heart,
it's as big as their western blue sky.
It's far more kinder and understanding
and always ready to comfort most anyone's cry.

TO RIDE THE OLD WEST AGAIN

Now if you want To Ride The Old West Again
just close your eyes and dream
and let your heart begin to listen
and you'll hear its wild horses' scream.

You'll hear the sounds of gunfire
and see the James Boys ride by.
You'll watch its great cattle drives
and hear Custer's dying cry.

You'll smell its millions of buffalo
and feel the earth tremble as they thunder by.
You'll see the west as it once was
and hear the first wagon masters' westward cry.

You'll see great visions of its endless distance
and virgin mountains that once touched virgin skies.
You'll even see the mounted Calvary charge
and hear the Indians' waring battle cry.

You'll taste the pureness of its youth
and hear her first train's coming cry.
You'll see the bleached bones of its first dreamers
right where each one of them long ago did die.

So, if you want To Ride The Old West Again
just close your eyes and dream
and let your heart begin to listen
and you'll hear its wild horses' scream.

WOLF SONGS

Let the wolves once again cry I say.
Let them freely roam God's natural intended way.
Let their songs our souls to our high mountains lift.
Let their voices within our western valleys once again drift.

Put them back where they belong.
Let them again sing their wilderness song.
Let us see their tracks in a winter's fallen snow.
Let their eyes once again within our western moonlight glow.

Let them live their given way.
Let them under our big sky stray.
Let us each remember and each understand
that they lived here long before us in this God-given land.

So, let the wolves once again cry I say.
Let them freely roam, God's natural intended way.
Let their songs, our souls to our high mountains lift.
Let their voices within our western valleys once again drift.

THE SLIGHTEST CLUE

Now some say us Montanans are downright Big Sky crazy
that our souls are overflowing with its pure waters of blue
that our every thought is lost within its mountainous beauty
and as to why they say they don't have The Slightest Clue.

But you see, we understand the real depth of our chosen way.
Our Montanan hearts hear its every wind-whispered song.
We each feel the soft touch of its living breath every day
and for its western peace and many gifts we each daily long.

But then some say us Montanans are downright Big Sky crazy
that our souls are overflowing with its pure waters of blue
that our every thought is lost within its mountainous beauty
so, isn't it a shame they don't even have The Slightest Clue?

CRYSTAL STREAMS

Within my sometimes nightly dreams
I often hear the gentle songs of Montana's Crystal Streams.
Their many singing voices fill my thirsty listening soul.
Their living words to my heart, endless old stories have told.

Stories from long before the first white man,
when this land was still free, open and pure.
Stories of its first born
who long ago learned this land to love and endure.

Stories of its many animals,
more than all Africa has ever known.
Stories of their great living value
long before the evil seeds of gun powder were sown.

Stories of its first stillness,
when only the wind's young voice was heard.
Stories from its first given day,
eons before the birth of the spoken human word.

Stories of great eternal meaning
mixed within the blowing winds of time.
All stories carried in the hearts of angels
who still fly above this special land, gentle and kind.

For within my sometimes nightly dreams,
I often hear the gentle songs of Montana's Crystal Streams.
Their many singing voices fill my thirsty listening soul.
Their living words, to my heart, endless old stories have told.

BRIGHT WESTERN BLUE

Below the broadness of Montana's big sky
summer-colored, Bright Western Blue
lies a vast and rugged land of wilderness beauty
made by God and His hard-working, angel crew.

You'll discover a rugged land of many mountains,
trout filled rivers and beautiful pure streams.
A shining place to live and die;
a land of hope for our own human dreams.

The gift of deep stillness is found in Montana
that allows one to hear on its winds, God's gentle voice.
A place where our human souls can find the rest they need
and of its endless wonders, in our nightly prayers, rejoice.

Solid proof of Heaven is found everywhere you look
that our Creator, so long ago, lovingly left behind.
His many gifts, His many treasures for us all to enjoy;
a loving Father's caring and lasting living sign.

For below the broadness of Montana's big sky
summer-colored, Bright Western Blue
lies a vast and rugged land of wilderness beauty
made by God and His hard-working, angel crew.

IN THIS MONTANA LAND

In This Montana Land, where the western meadowlark flies
and summer-cotton clouds gently float in liquid-blue skies,
you can still see the buffalo from long, long ago,
and its evening sunsets will set your heart and soul all aglow.

Its summer mountains lie bright in last winter's melting snow
while deep in its green valleys the winds of July warmly blow.
This season runs hard, dry and the color of dusty earth brown.
It's where the nesting cries of wild eagles are so easily found.

Its people are special hard workers, strong and kind.
They're some of the nicest you'll ever meet or find.
They know of the deep value of the land on which they live
and back to it, their blood, sweat and tears they freely give.

For In This Montana Land the western meadowlark flies
and summer-cotton clouds gently float in liquid-blue skies.
You can still see the buffalo from long, long ago
and find sunsets that will set your heart and soul all aglow.

MONTANA DAYDREAMERS

Montana Daydreamers are found on its every mountain high.
They're seen looking into its deep blue painted Indian sky.
You'll find them skiing on winter snows of diamond crystal white.
You'll find them in its forests full of soft emerald light.

You'll find them listening to a bull elk's September's cry,
for their souls know where all of Montana's wonders lie.
You'll find them throughout its vastness tasting its very best,
for they've learned how to use it; how to use its perfect rest.

They're found within the western poet's written poetic words.
They sing Indian songs and weep for its past buffalo herds.
They're found within each human heart who calls Montana home.
They're found watching eagles fly that within its skies roam.

They're found fishing in its streams that run toward the sea.
They're found dreaming in the shade of river cottonwood trees.
They're found standing in its fields of flowers each new spring.
They're found counting birds that nest there and sing.

For Montana Daydreamers are found on its every mountain high.
They're found looking into its deep blue painted Indian sky.
They're found skiing on winter snows of diamond crystal-white.
They're found throughout all its forests full of soft emerald wilderness light.

BY HEAVEN'S HAND

Like the finest wine
is this beautiful Montana land.
Rare and well-aged she is
long-ago bottled by Heaven's Hand.

MONTANA BOUND

I'm packing it in now
and leaving this dirty and dying, big city town.
You see, I'm heading west early tomorrow.
Thank God, I'm now Montana Bound.

For I hear its wilderness voice calling to me
in every picture of Montana I see.
I want to live within its vastness
where the air is still pure and pollution-free.

I want to drink from its icy cold mountain streams,
and beneath its nightly stars, I want to sleep and easily dream.
I want to cleanse my soul; to renew it once again.
I want to taste its pine-scented, snowy winter wind.

I want to live where God's angels still daily fly,
and touch the color of its famous blue cowboy sky.
I want to learn all about what real silence really means.
I want to let my heart feed on its famous sunset scenes.

So that's why I'm packing it in now
and leaving this dirty and dying, big city town,
For I'm heading west early tomorrow.
Thank God, I'm now Montana Bound.

WHERE THE RIVERS RUN TOWARD HEAVEN CLEAR

To live Where The Rivers Run Toward Heaven Clear
to hunt in a land full of trophy deer
to walk where wild eagles always fly
to drink in the pureness of a Montana big sky.

For I live Where The Rivers Run Toward Heaven Clear.
I hunt in a land full of trophy deer.
I daily walk where wild eagles always fly.
I drink in the pureness of a Montana big sky.

So, if you want to live Where The Rivers Run Toward Heaven Clear
if you want to hunt in a land full of trophy deer
if you want to walk where wild eagles always fly
then you need to drink in the pureness of a Montana big sky.

DREAMING OF MONTANA

To fly with its soaring eagles.
To dream their fierce hunter dreams.
To climb its high rugged mountains.
To drink the pureness of its cold flowing streams.

To hunt its majestic bull elk
through the softness of a fresh tracking snow.
To enjoy the company of fellow hunters
by the wilderness warmth of a fire's light, November glow.

To rise early before dawn's coming light
to the smells of frying bacon and coffee cups of rising steam.
I'm dreaming of going to Montana every night now.
I'm dreaming of someday soaring with its eagles.
To someday dream their fierce hunter dreams.

OUR MONTANA PLACE

The very touch of Heaven
still lies upon Our Montana Place;
from our vast eastern wind-swept prairie
to our western mountains winter-topped with snowy angel lace.

We're daily blessed with her pine-scented air
that's still Eden-fresh and blue-sky clear.
And each fall we enjoy our many wilderness fruits
of our elusive elk and mule and whitetail deer.

Our many rivers still race wild and deep, icy cold,
each home to hungry trout that always fight, line-snapping bold.
Our skies still carry the wild sounds of eagle screams.
Our land still remembers every spoken Indian dream.

We're still a forgiving and rugged kind of people.
Hardworking and a fair cut above our winter's given best.
For we're proud Montanans blessed to live in this place
where God still comes to seek His daily rest.

A SOLEMN DAY'S AIR

Bury this soldier gently.
Bury this soldier deep.
Bury this soldier with honor.
Fold the flag for those who weep.

Remember him with kindness.
Remember his youthful smile.
Remember his brave willingness
to walk the soldier's last mile.

Fire each salvo with reverence.
Fire each salvo with care.
Fire each salvo toward Heaven
bringing thunder to A Solemn Day's Air.

So, bury this soldier gently.
Bury this soldier deep.
Bury this soldier with honor.
Fold the flag for those who weep.

PROMISES

Over the years there are many Promises we've kept
and some Promises, regrettably, we've broken.
There are many Promises we've yet to dream
and always those silent Promises of ours, yet unspoken.

RUNNING WILD, RUNNING FREE

I've seen him Running Wild, Running Free.
I've seen him running under a river-green, cottonwood tree.
I've heard his bugle on a frosty fall morning's first light.
I've found his shed antlers, still brown or ivory white.

I've seen him and other seeking-bulls savagely fight.
I've seen his raw power; I've seen his wilderness might.
I've seen deep inside his wild western soul.
I've found him to be brave and kingly bold.

For I've seen him Running Wild, Running Free.
I've seen him running under a river-green, cottonwood tree.
I've heard his bugle on a frosty fall morning's first light.
I've even found his shed antlers, still brown or ivory white.

WHY?

Why is Montana
so special, so nice?
Why do her many rivers
flow with liquid ice?

Why are there so many eagles
in her skies of robin-egg blue?
Why are all her lands
like a vast outdoor zoo?

Why is she famous
for her sunsets; her trout-filled streams?
Why is she the fulfiller
of so many of our human dreams?

Why are her many mountains
so tall, so beautiful to see?
Why is she the only place left
that contains Heaven's unlocking key?

Why are her people
so brave, so western-bold?
Why are her snowy winters
so long, so remembered cold?

Why is she known now
as The Last Best Place?
Why do summers bring drought
and wild fires that race?

So Why is Montana
so special, so nice?
I guess it's because
she has the gift to our souls entice?

CHRISTMAS STAR

Christmas Star over Montana's snowy mountains
Its light shimmering diamond-bright
Shutting out all the stars of Heaven
Ruling all the sky that one special night.

MANKIND'S METAL TRAPS OF TEARS

Bobcat I've seen a-running;
running over ice and snow
seeking to kill its meal
with a savage razor-like blow.

Livin' deep in the woods
far from the angry eyes of man,
summer footprints I've found
by hidden stream's, soft wet sand.

Living like a ghostly shadow;
only man's city smell he fears.
Sadly, he's slowly disappearing from our lands
done in by Mankind's Metal Traps Of Tears.

For Bobcat I've seen a-running.
I've seen it running on winter's ice and snow.
I've watched it quickly kill its meal
with its savage razor-like blow.

THE LAST BEST PLACE

Beyond the crowded and dying cities of modern man
lies a special land of soft blue skies;
a big land of eternal western beauty;
God's Eden of forever wild eagle cries.

It can be found sometimes within your starless sleeping dreams,
or by following a moon beam on a cool summer's night.
It's full of wild elk and mighty grizzly bears,
and snowy mountains, each of Heaven's chosen height.

It's a land of endless soft spring rainbows;
a place where you can still find life's golden key.
A land of western vastness so deep, so lasting wide
that it sets most human souls flying toward heaven free.

It's well known now as The Last Best Place;
a land still full of real wilderness grace.
Its winters are deep snowy; its summers white-bone dry.
It's the only place on the earth where real angels fly.

So, learn to look beyond the dying and crowded cities of man.
Look and you'll see this Montana land is still full of soft blue skies,
for it's only in The Last Best Place, my friend,
where one can still hear its forever wild eagle cries.

HER WILD WESTERN SKY

Deep below Her Wild Western Sky
the true pureness of Heaven's beauty lies;
a beauty far beyond the mere works of mortal man;
a God-touched land of high mountains and wind-blown sand;

A vastness of eternal wilderness every piece Heaven bound;
a place of savage winter winds and echoing eagle sounds;
a land full of soul food, it'll even change the way one thinks;
full of sunrises and sunsets, each cloud painted orange to pink.

Its summers are hot and dead-bone desert dry.
Its winters are deep cold and full of snow-white skies.
Its people are western-brave and made Montana-bold.
Their lives run with its two seasons, plain-hot and hard-cold.

Its animals are many; they're the living spirit of all its lands
created to winter feed the bloody force of man's hunting hands.
Its many rivers flow the raw power of fresh liquid ice.
Its towering mountain pines sway and dance, to our eyes entice.

For deep below Her Wild Western Sky
the true pureness of Heaven's beauty lies;
a beauty far beyond the mere works of mortal man;
For it's a God-touched land of high mountains and wind-blown sand.

SWEET WATER MEMORIES

My heart and soul are full of Sweet Water Memories,
memories of a western land called The Last Best Place,
fond memories of its many different kinds of people,
people of every type from our ever-expanding human race.

Memories of a vastness that changed my soul forever more,
memories of sunsets that God painted to feed my heart each night,
memories of those night skies with stars, each diamond-bright,
memories of sunrises full of new promises and soft new daylight.

Memories of its long western winters, deep and bad-guy mean,
memories of its mighty mountain grizzly and black bears,
memories of its almost uncountable kinds of hawks and eagles,
memories of a land that all the gifts of heaven still bears.

For my heart and soul are full of Sweet Water Memories,
memories of a real land now called The Last Best Place,
very fond memories of its many different kinds of people,
good people of every type from our ever-expanding human race.

SOLDIER BOY - SOLDIER MAN

Soldier Boy, Soldier Man
why do you now cry?
I cry because I just saw
my best friend die.

Soldier Boy, Soldier Man
how did he just die?
It was an unseen sniper
that caused him in death to now lie.

Soldier Boy, Soldier Man
what will you now do?
Into a body bag I will place him
since his life here is now forever through.

Soldier Boy, Soldier Man
how do you now feel?
Great lasting anger
I wonder if this hurt will ever heal?

Soldier Boy, Soldier Man
to his family will a letter you now write?
Oh yes, yes
at the rising of tomorrow's renewing first light.

So then Soldier Boy, Soldier Man
why do you still so deeply cry?
Because today I just saw
my best friend and only brother die.

THE WANNABE KID

I wannabe good
but sometimes I wannabe bad.
I always wannabe happy
and never wannabe sad.

I wannabe loved.
I wannabe liked.
I wannabe forever young,
and someday ride a two-wheeler bike.

I wannabe rich.
I wannabe clever.
I wannabe smart,
and grow old, well never.

I wannabe strong.
I wannabe a best friend.
I wannabe a super hero,
and bars of steel bend.

For I wannabe good
but sometimes I wannabe bad.
I always wannabe happy,
and never ever wannabe sad.

BROTHERS ONE

We're blood brothers each
Born under the same living sun
Born of different seen colors
But born of Heaven's hand to be as Brothers One.

For we were born to care, to share, to see
Born to accept each other, racism free
Born to help, to know, to dare
Born to love each other, for each other to care.

Born to teach, to plant, to reap
Born to God's commandments to cherish and keep
Born to help the widow, the infirm, the unborn
Born to share another's burdens when another mourns.

For we are blood brothers each
Born under the same living sun
Born of different seen colors
But born of Heaven's hand to be as Brothers One.

SUNDAY BOOTS

I pray that when I someday die
upon my favorite saddle blanket I'll peacefully lie
with my best Sunday Boots all shiny and neat,
lovingly placed upon this departed old cowboy's feet.

For you see, I've grown old now and somewhat tired,
been many long years since I retired,
but I'm still branding a few calves every new spring,
and playing my old guitar and doing those common cowboy things.

I'm more than well-weathered, that's for sure.
You see I've spent my entire life livin' hard and cowboy-pure.
I even shot a few bad guys to stay alive;
me and my Colt, we've long this western life survived.

Now I've owned many a horse in my livin' time
and some were mean as hell and some were fast and western-fine.
And I've watched this west change before my very eyes.
I've seen my share of God's rainbows within its stormy skies.

I guess I've just about roped and branded
most every range cow that was ever western born,
and when I think about the good old days,
well, my old eyes get kind of misty and really forlorn.

But I've had a good long life working and riding the west.
I lived it to its fullest, to do my very cowboy-best.
Now I wouldn't trade it for nothing, no sir-ee,
for I lived it as lucky as a cowboy could ever want it to be.

But you see, I've now grown old and somewhat tired
been many long years since I retired.
But I'm still branding a few calves every new spring,
and playing my old guitar and doing those common cowboy things.

So, I nightly pray that when I someday die
upon my favorite saddle blanket I'll peacefully lie
with my best Sunday Boots all shiny and neat,
lovingly placed upon this departed old cowboy's feet.

WESTERN GLORY

Western Glory
upon Montana's high mountains lie.
Heaven's crystal pureness is found here
throughout all of its vast big sky.

Harsh winter storms come
bringing snow for its next summer of "the long dry;"
endless fields of blooming wild flowers
lie everywhere, beneath its warming spring skies.

Howling wolves again roam here
in its towering forests of virgin wilderness green.
Battling bull elk are heard
in the early days of fall before winter's snowy scenes.

Song birds seen fleeing south
long before the breath of December arrives.
A toughness of the human soul needed
for this land's long winter to survive.

Endless amounts of split firewood;
each piece stacked with remembered sweat and care.
A golden eagle seen flying overhead
a moment in time so special and rare.

Firelight casting its needed warmth
from an oil lamp lit at night.
Watching its stars of distant brilliance
tasting the gift of their given light.

Fishing alone on a rushing wild river
while the winds of time blow
Basking in the evening softness
of one of its September sunsets aglow

Skiing downhill on fresh fallen powder
Watching the world without a care, rush by
Of life's lasting value and true soul worth
To be gained here, under its ocean deep, blue sky

For true Western Glory you'll find here
Upon all of Montana it lies
For Heaven's crystal pureness is found throughout
Throughout all of its vast and unforgettable big sky

THE FIRST PURENESS

What eternal gift does this land of Montana
to each searching human soul bear?
What special gift does it possess
that makes it so unique and so earthly rare?

Is it because some have called it
The Last Best Place
Where one can still find the needed relief
from our ever-expanding human race?

Might it be because its high mountain meadows
still flow with The First Pureness of Heaven's given streams?
Or is it because it's known to hold for each truth seeker
the answers to their own soul-searching dreams?

Or just maybe it's because its vast wilderness lands
still echo with the sounds its long-ago birthing cry?
Or is it because as some have found out
that within its Eden spirit the door of Heaven lies?

So just what eternal gift does this land of Montana
to each searching human soul bear?
Just what special gift does it possess
that makes it so unique and still so earthly rare?

THIS PLACE CALLED MONTANA

God bless This Place Called Montana.
God bless all her given lands.
God bless all who love her.
God bless every Montanan's hard-working hands.

God bless her many lived freedoms.
God bless the wilderness spirit she bears.
God bless her many crystal rivers.
God bless all her outdoor gifts she shares.

God bless all her fallen heroes.
God bless them forever more.
God bless her future.
God bless all her eagles, who just below Heaven soar.

So, God bless This Place Called Montana.
God bless all her given lands.
God bless all who love her.
God bless every Montanan's hard-working hands.

IN THE LAND OF HEAVEN'S GLORY

In The Land Of Heaven's Glory
there lies an endless, eternal western story;
a story so deep, so Eden-fresh and true.
It's the story of why Montana's sky is still so pure-water blue.

You see Montana was the first place that God ever made;
when He made our earth and its trees and their cooling shade.
That's why He still comes here to rest and pray
and why the songs of His angels are still heard here every day.

For they're heard in every sunrise and every sunset too.
They're heard throughout its mountainous sky, in peaceful blue.
They're heard in the giant pine, wind-singing trees.
They're heard everywhere, for one's searching soul to please.

They're heard in its stars that shine crystal bright.
They're heard in its many waters that sparkle at night.
They're heard in the heartbeats of those who love its land.
They're heard in flowered fields where buffalo once ran.

They're heard by its eagles who fly free in its sky.
They're heard by its bears who sleep in mountain caves up high.
They're heard by its mighty elk and far ranging deer.
They're heard by all things who have the heart to hear.

For in this wondrous Land Of Heaven's glory
there lies an endless, eternal western story;
a story so deep, so Eden-fresh and true.
It's the story of why Montana's sky is still so pure-water blue.

For Montana was the first place that God ever made
when He made our earth and its trees and their cooling shade.
It's where He still comes to daily rest and pray.
That's why the songs of His angels are still heard here today.

THOSE COWBOY HANDS

He has Those Cowboy Hands.
They're as rugged and strong as an old western pine.
They're deep-weathered, calloused and rope-burned scarred.
They're one of the surest of a hard-working cowboy's sign.

They were never made for washing no woman's china dishes,
or painting a house or planting a fancy flower garden or two.
No, those cowboy hands he has were made for breaking wild horses
and branding and working cattle the whole night through.

They were made for starting and stopping barroom fights,
and saving a new calf from a late winter's deep snowstorm;
for roping, mending fences, and rodeo riding
and for splitting wood to keep the bunkhouse warm.

They were made for setting endless miles of fence posts
and skinning every kind of wild western game;
for shoeing fresh-broke horses
and rubbing on liniment when they came up lame.

They were made for building line shacks, making horse hair ropes,
and digging deep into the earth, looking for a sweet-water well,
and they were made ready and always willing
to send any horse-whipping, mean son-of-a-gun straight to hell.

So, look for Those Cowboy Hands the next time you see one.
They'll be as rugged and strong as an old western pine.
They'll be deep-weathered, calloused and rope-burned scarred.
They'll be one of the surest of a hard-working cowboy's sign.

MONTANA SPRING

In Montana
when the spring winds finally blow
You'll find her mountains and valleys
full of Heaven's wild flowers aglow

You'll find her skies full of bluebirds and robins
Her cottonwood trees returning to a remembered green
Her mountain snowline rushing ever upward
Her sunsets as fresh and rich as homemade ice cream

Her rivers and streams will be rushing ice-water cold
and wild eagles will be seen nesting in her trees
Her deer and elk will have shed their antlers
to be gathered up and shipped to other lands overseas

Her people will have a renewed sparkle in their eyes
and from within them, you'll hear a long held, winter sigh
And in her returning Spring rainbows you'll often hear
the red-tailed hawks' sky-diving, mating cry

For in this season of Montana
when spring winds finally blow
You'll find her every mountain, her every valley
full of Heaven's wild flowers aglow

THE MOUNTAINS OF MY DREAMS

In the land of the Bitterroots and shining Sapphires
In that place of my found western dreams
There lies a valley paradise and high snowy mountains
A place richly full of wild Montana eagle screams

It's a rugged place of many treasures
A place of towering western trees
A birthing land for double summer rainbows
A place that one's lonely soul can so easily be free

Its very earth is daily Heaven-blessed
Its rushing streams are cold and liquid ice pure
Its air is crystal fresh and the west's finest
Its wilderness spirit, a wounded heart can so quickly cure

For in the land of my Bitterroots and shining Sapphires
In this place of my own found western dreams
There lies a valley paradise and high snowy mountains
My home, so richly full of wild Montana eagle screams

THE SECOND SKY

There's a distant place I know of
It lies far above all the earth's land and deep-water seas
A paradise widely known as The Second Sky
It's where all the good cowboys go to live fence-fixing free

You'll find it full of flying eagles
It's where the wind-breath of God gently blows
A place of eternal peace and fresh spring skies
That place where all the many fruits of Heaven grow

Now you can often see it reflected
in the west's endless lakes and high mountain streams
For The Second Sky is the giver
of all the poetic thoughts of every cowboy poet's written dreams

For there really exists a distant place I know of
It lies far above all our earth's land and deep-water seas
It's a paradise widely known as The Second Sky
It's where all the good cowboys go to live fence-fixing free

MONTANA IS

Montana Is rain and drought
Where double rainbows fly
It is lightning and forest fires
Where wild eagles live and die

It is Indians and abandoned stone circles
Where the shaggy buffalo still run
It is high snowy mountains
Where winter's only relief is a summer's blazing sun

It is elk and deer and cougar
Where the past is sought in journey dreams
It is sweet sage brush and towering pines
Where grizzly prints lie fresh by high valley streams

It's a vastness and wildness
Where the heart of the earth lies
It is majestic sunsets and howling wolves
Where diamonds fill or grace the nightly skies

For Montana Is rain and drought
Where double rainbows fly
It is lightning and forest fires
Where wild eagles live and die

THE MONTANA MAN

The Montana Man
stands tall and strong
His western heart overflowing
with its vast wilderness song

His eyes reflect the deep color
of his land's endless blue sky
His rugged Montana soul hears
every wild eagle cry

His hands are tough and weathered
as the bark of an old yellow pine
He stands unique and all alone
He's a rare breed, one-of-a-kind

His backbone is made of granite
it's as strong as the Montana mountains he loves
His cowboy hat is faded and long-stained
and blood will be on his working gloves

His horse is as fast as the summer wind
No stray cow can match its blinding speed
For he stands unique and all alone
He's one-of-a-kind; a man of rare western breed

HOPEFUL DREAMS

Oh, Montana woman
with eyes of saddle brown
Deep within them I see
an endless love for this western ground

Oh, Montana woman
with eyes of new summer green
Deep within them I see
a thirst for this land's high mountain streams

Oh, Montana woman
with eyes of big sky blue
Deep within them I see
a longing for this land's pureness, wilderness true

Oh, Montana woman
with eyes of wild wolf gray
Deep within them I see
the need for riding horses every given day

Oh, Montana woman
with eyes of hazel, so beautiful so clear
Deep within them I see
summer rainbows and high plains deer

Oh, Montana women
with eyes full of soaring eagle screams
Deep within them all I see
a western radiance of your many Hopeful Dreams

THE ENDLESS BIG BLUE

This Montana place
This land of transforming sky
This land that has lassoed and branded my soul
This place where my wind-blown ashes will someday lie

So vast of western beauty it is
So overwhelmingly full of The Endless Big Blue
So life-changing to everyone
To everyone who its western lands pass through

Bearer of skies full of flying eagles
Keeper of flowing waters, cold and crystal clear
For each drop it has collected over the eons of time
Collected to form its many waters of Heaven's fallen tears

Birthplace of racing rainbows
Land of snowy mountains of gentle worth
Guardian of the doorway to eternity
The place where God awaits each one's rebirth

Oh, this Montana place
Oh, land transforming sky
Oh, land that has lassoed and branded my soul
It's here where my wind-blown ashes will someday lie

BIG SKIES OF LIVING WESTERN BLUE

Montana, have I told you lately that I love you?
Have I told you lately just how much I care?
Have I told you you're my heart's only desire?
That your land is so special and western rare?

Have I thanked you lately for your mighty mountains?
So majestic and so crystal snowy high.
Have I thanked you for your forests
that throughout all your vastness in wildness still lie?

Have I thanked you for your pure rushing rivers
that run icy-cold and shining diamond-clear?
Have I thanked you for softness of your fresh air
and the enjoyed beauty of your many seen deer?

Have I thanked you lately for your cowboys and your ranches
that still hold to the western way, each honor true?
Have I told you lately that you hold our hearts spellbound
with your Big Skies Of Living Western Blue?

So, Montana, have I told you lately that I love you?
Have I told you lately just how much I really care?
Have I told you lately you're my heart's only true desire?
That your land is so special and truly western-rare?

WHERE WILD EAGLES DON'T FLY

Don't go Montana child
Where Wild Eagles Don't Fly
Don't leave your birthland behind
Don't go where you can't hear their wilderness cry

Don't look to other distant pastures
Now so full of the tempting sounds of a big city's neon cry
Don't go Montana child
Where Wild Eagles Don't Fly

Don't travel the downward path of self-serving thoughts
For someday, and all alone in deep sadness, you'll die
Don't go Montana child
Where Wild Eagles Don't Fly

Don't listen to the foolish dreams of the proud, the lost
For they care not for the sounds of your birthland's cry
Don't go Montana child
Where Wild Eagles Don't Fly

Seek to stay here Montana child
To live the fullness where wild Montana eagles always fly
Don't leave your birthland behind my child
Don't go where you can't hear their wilderness cry

THE WHITE BUFFALO

Oh, Montana of modern day
Keeper of crystal skies still so deep, so wilderness-blue
Home to the spirit of The White Buffalo
Within your vast western soul he still thunders through

Guardian of your many waters, blood to your dry land
Flowing over your ancient bedrock and thirsty sage brush sand
Builder of your tall mountains where your wild eagles fly
He's sometimes summer seen, running through white-cloud sky

Sacred to the ones who once ruled all your land
Long since oppressed by the force of the man's hand
Bearer of your seasons; from his breath the four winds blow
Provider of your winter rains that fall as your mountain snow

Catcher of the dreams and songs of your past
Held visions of painted faces, war hoops, horses running fast
Watcher of all tepees, the strength to each bow-maker's hands
The spirit of The White Buffalo still roams your lands

Oh, my Montana of modern day
Keeper of crystal skies still so deep, so wilderness-blue
You are home to the spirit of The White Buffalo
Listen to your western soul, for he still thunders through

WILD MONTANA HEART

I've got a Wild Montana Heart now
beating deep within my chest
Beating to the pulse of this wondrous land
that now gives my soul and pen little rest

Racing like a fleeing deer
it daily fills me with flying eagle screams
Sending my every thought outward
to travel along this land's high mountain streams

It has filled me with endless joy and wonderment
ever since it first heard the spirit of this land softly sing
For it understands its every spoken word now
and to its every thought my soul and I breathlessly cling

Now forever lost deep within this land's vastness
our spirits have joined to become as one
From Montana's new day's first-seen rising light
To the day ending glory of its setting western sun

For you see you've got a Wild Montana Heart
now beating deep within my pounding chest.
Beating to the pulse of this wondrous land
that now gives my soul and pen little rest

SOUL MEDICINE

Blue birds and singing angels
and a wild-flowered Montana spring
will take away the sadness from any human soul
and make it once again laugh and sing

MONTANA BLUE

I've found a place
where eagles and angels fly
A place of answered dreams
and endless western sky

I thought it only existed
within my own human dreams
Until one remembered day of long ago
when I first heard one of its flying eagles scream

Now, since that day, my life has changed
For I now live within its vast Sapphire range
A range of shining mountains under its pure western sky
A place where I've seen resting eagles and angels lie

Now some call this land The Last Best Place
Where the human soul of Heaven's glory can touch and taste
A place of lasting richness, so deep, so true
A place of cowboy skies always colored Montana Blue

TOWARD CHERRY RED

Montana's winter winds now howling
with snow so stinging white
Howling down from the north they come
with blizzard arctic might.

Our woodstove's glowing Toward Cherry Red
to keep the numbing cold at bay
When will this deep coldness pass
that keeps our sun's warmth away?

We're dreaming all the time now
of the remembered days from our summer past
We pray its memories will keep us sane
as into our hungry woodstoves more wood we cast.

For nothing now moves in this great white stillness
These arctic winds scream like some hellish beast alive
Our woodstove is glowing Toward Cherry Red
Lord, will spring again here arrive?

For Montana's winter winds now howling
with snow so stinging white
Howling down from the north they come
with blizzard arctic might.

OUR SHARED HOPES
WE CAST

We're Montanans one and all
A mix of human colors; some short, some tall
We each bear her future; we've each born her past
Upon the current millennium, Our Shared Hopes We Cast

WIND DREAMS

In the dawn of a Montana's early light
I've seen its endless stars fade away from diamond-bright
I've watched a full moon fall behind its snowy mountain scene
I've cherished every sunset and heard the voices of Wind Dreams

I've listened to the singing of its crystal waterfalls
and heard on its emerald lakes distant soul-piercing loon calls
I've seen its elk in the fall, fight to keep alive their seed
and watched wild geese in a moonlit field feed

I've loved this land for many a year
and more than once felt the wetness from a falling angel's tears
I've seen its winter sky turn angry and icy-mean
and heard the pleading cry of a hunted rabbit's dying scream

I've felt the very presence of Heaven in its endless sky
and watched white dragon clouds in its summer's heat float by
I've tasted the cold pureness of its many crystal streams
and flown with its wild eagles within my own daily dreams

For in the dawn of a Montana's early light
I've seen its endless stars fade away from diamond-bright
I've watched a full moon fall behind its snowy mountain scene
I've cherished every sunset and heard the voices of Wind Dreams

THIS WONDROUS EDEN

How high is it to the top of Montana's Big Sky
where wild eagles still live and hunt and die?
How fresh is the air that fills its endless lands
where the work of God is still ongoing in its sagebrush lands?

How pure is the water born by the western winds
that feeds its many rivers full of trout with spotted fins?
How bright are the stars that shine at night
that fills all its lands with a heavenly light?

How tall are the pines that hold up the blue sky
that watch its wild wolves when they run by?
How beautiful is the spring when its wild flowers grow
that are tended by angels under God's loving glow?

But just how long will This Wondrous Eden last
if people keep moving here into new houses from concrete cast?
Will Montana still be the same a hundred years from now
or will it have then perished under the bulldozer's plow?

So, just how high is it to the top of Montana's Big Sky
where wild eagles still live and hunt and die?
And just how fresh is the air that fills its endless lands
where the work of God is still ongoing, in its sagebrush lands?

THESE HEAVENS ABOVE

High up in Montana's eagle-filled sky
Far, far above where the snowy mountains lie,
You'll find that place where angels always sing
You'll find the promised land of God's eternal spring

It contains a real softness in each day's glow
and a lasting peace that we don't yet know
A place empty of all pain, sorrows and human fear
A place of brilliant blue skies always storm-cloud clear

There's a golden gate where old friends await
Children and grandparents and each one's mate
Its living waters spring forth cold and crystal-pure
From all your felt sadness these waters will someday cure

For its high up in Montana's eagle-filled sky
Far, far above where its snowy mountains lie,
You'll find that place where angels always sing
You'll find that promised land of God's eternal spring

MONTANA EMOTIONS

I've seen its mountains at first light shine
I've heard its snowflakes fall, gentle and winter-kind
I've tasted its rainbows all bright and raindrop-clear
I've walked its vast lands so full of wild, bounding deer

I've daydreamed by its streams each cold and pure
I've let it, my heart, fix and cure
I've nightly watched its stars shine diamond-bright
I've daily basked in its every sunset's healing light

I've come to understand just what Montana to me, really means
I've discovered here a foretaste of Heaven's coming scenes
I've learned that angels within its Big Sky still daily sing
I've seen the very touch of God in its wildflowers of spring

For I live to see its mountains at first light shine
I live to hear its snowflakes fall, gentle and winter-kind
I live to taste its rainbows all bright and raindrop-clear
I live to walk its vast lands so full of wild, bounding deer

MONTANA COWBOYS

Now Montana Cowboys love their guns
They love their daughters and each born son
They love livin' their kind of rugged western life
They love their horses and their life-sharing wife

They love just about most everything
Like rodeo riding and old cowboy songs to sing
They love wild cattle to rope and brand
They love the vastness of Montana's open land

They love spending nights beneath crystal stars
They love pickup trucks instead of fancy city cars
They love the pureness of Montana's fresh mountain air
They love riding for the brand at fall's county fair

They're thankful for each God-given breath
They're not afraid to look at the face of death
They're a rare breed of rugged western man
Each special-molded from God's own branding hands

For all Montana Cowboys love their guns
They love their daughters and each born son
They love livin' their kind of rugged western life
They love their horses and their life-sharing wife

THE CLOUDS OF MONTANA

Saddles and spurs and worn dusty boots
Six-guns and Winchesters are every Montana cowboy's roots
Breaking horses, branding irons and barroom fights
Sleeping on the hard ground is their hard-earned nightly right

Tending fences, stretching wire
Watching the nightly heavens, talking to the stars
Playing cards, having too much to drink
Getting up early with The Clouds Of Montana painted pink

Blazing winter trails, riding the lands of endless room
Searching for lost cattle under the light of a hunter's moon
Working in the heat, hot enough to fry one's brains
Living as a part of Montana's great western range

For Montana cowboys are saddles and spurs and worn dusty boots
Blazing six-guns and Winchesters are their western roots
Breaking horses, branding irons and barroom fights
Sleeping on its hard ground is their hard-earned nightly right

MONTANA REASONS

There are no stars quite so bright
as all the stars seen in a Montana's winter's night
There's no air still so pure
as its air your soul will cure

There's no other place so beautiful or nice
where mountain waters still taste of liquid ice
There's no other sky so full of wild eagle screams
or any land that can fulfill all your secret dreams

There's no need here for the thoughts of worldly things
like fancy clothes or shiny diamond, golden rings
There's no rhyme or reason to rush or speed
For here you'll learn to relax, pray, and winter read

You see, there's a new you just waiting to be reborn
It'll happen your very first-tasted, fresh Montana morn
You'll hear the early rising beats of feathered angel wings
You'll hear all the voices of Heaven that first morning sing

There are no stars quite so bright
as all the stars seen in a Montana's winter's night
There's no air still so pure
as its air your soul will cure

OF FALLING WINTER LACE

To live in this Montana place
so full of Heaven's given grace
To write of its endless seen beauty
To feel upon my face its flakes Of Falling Winter Lace

To enjoy its blazing western sunsets
of orange and fading, remembered, day-ending grays
To drink from its refreshing crystal mountain waters
makes something special of each of its lived big sky days

To listen to its busy hummingbirds of spring
when all of Heaven's given flowers bloom
To watch all of this land's many animals
live wild and free within all of its endless wilderness room

To hear the nightly summer cry of a diving nighthawk
when all of the stars of Heaven upon it shine
To discover that this Montana land is but a foretaste
of something else coming, someday, far gentler and kind

For I love living in this Montana place
That's so full of Heaven's given grace
I love to write of its endless seen beauty
and to feel upon my face its flakes Of Falling Winter Lace

MONTANA MOMENT

It was a Montana Moment
when I first heard one of its wild eagles cry
It was a Montana Moment
when my soul learned to feed on its everywhere blue sky

It was a Montana Moment
when I realized this land and I had become as one
It was a Montana Moment
when my heart first tasted the wild spices in its setting sun

It was a Montana Moment
when my mind learned the true depth of winter's bitter cold
It was a Montana Moment
when I started hearing its ancient Indian songs of old

It was a Montana Moment
when I lost my human need for all this world's perishable things
It was a Montana Moment
that day I first heard its mountain tops in storm clouds sing

It was a Montana Moment
when this land started fulfilling my spirit's every need
It was a Montana Moment
when I discovered its wild flowers came from Heaven's seeds

It was a Montana Moment
when I realized it's here where I'll breathe my final breath
It was a Montana Moment
when I found Heaven's door; that door just beyond the door of death

MY FATHER'S HANDS

High above Montana's deep blue skies
Far above its rugged western lands
Fly great wild hunting eagles
Long ago designed by My Father's Hands

Each carries a defiant look
rooted deep within their ever-searching eyes
All eagles seen flying
throughout this land's vast western skies

Their cries awaken ancient memories
of another distant time, of another distant place
Memories of long before our expanding and dying cities
now so full of death without the hand of Heaven's grace

A distant time when all of this land's water
flowed pure and humankind clear
When all its forests were endless and virgin
and had never once heard the sound of a falling human tear

A time when the only sounds
came from nature's birthing womb
When all creatures of this place
roamed fearless upon its lands and waters of endless room

For its here high above in Montana's deep blue skies
Far, far above its rugged western lands
Where great hunting eagles still freely fly
So long ago designed by My Father's Hands

ODE TO THE MONTANA WIND

Oh, Montana wind
can you hear my heart's whispered plea?
Carrier of scented pine and purple sagebrush
Guardian to Heaven's angels who hold its golden key

Watcher of this land's living rivers
Each running cold and western free
Oh, Montana wind
can you hear my heart's whispered plea?

Deliverer of winter's harsh, icy breath
Scatterer of our ashes after the touch of death
Lifter of earth from a passing summer storm
Oh, Montana wind, from our rugged mountains you're born

Pusher of wild geese
flying high in a fall's frosty night
Bender of our raindrops
found within our rainbows of remembered light

Mover of trees and our children's soaring kites
Builder of waves on our lakes on a hot summer's night
Protector of our eagles, flying wild and free
Oh, Montana wind, can you hear my heart's whispered plea?

Catcher of our human dreams
cast within your windy reach
Oh, Montana wind
please send them on to Heaven, to you, I beseech

OLD MAN WINTER

There's snow on our Montana ground
There's snow in our Montana air
Looks like Old Man Winter is combing out
all the dandruff in his snow-white cowboy hair

WAPITI

He lives and dies beneath the western sun
The tips of his antlers shine toward ivory white
Wapiti is his Indian name
The remembrance of his bugle heard in a fall's first light

Royal and majestic he stands all alone
That in which great hunting legends grow
Lives the west's mighty bull elk
Who fights each fall for his wild seeds to sow

Elusive as an evening's soft wind
He fears only the silent mountain lion's hunting eyes
Royal and majestic he stands all alone
Living and dying beneath the west's rugged wilderness skies

He once roamed in unchecked wild freedom
From the pacific shores, to our distant great eastern sea
Wapiti is his Indian name
The remembrance of his bugle heard sets the human soul free

For he's as elusive as an evening's soft wind
He fears only the silent mountain lion's hunting eyes
Royal and majestic he stands all alone
Living and dying beneath the west's rugged wilderness skies

WILD AND FREE

If I had but only one wish in my life
I know just what my wish would be
I'd wish to be a mighty Montana eagle
and fly far above its vastness, Wild And Free

I'd fly through its crystal pure mountain air
and catch only fresh trout for my every meal
I'd fly high enough to see the face of God
and from His many rainbows, their colors my eyes would steal

I'd fly through its sometimes-gray summer smoke
when the wild fires rage in fiery western bloom
I'd fly and soar across all its lands
where the heart can still find its needed breathing room

So, if I had only one wish in my life
I know just what my wish would be
I'd wish to be a mighty Montana eagle
and forever fly far above its vastness, Wild And Free

TRAILS END

At Trails End lies the promised land of milk and honey
At Trails End stands the doorway to eternal life
At Trails End grows the sweet grasses of Heaven
and its endless days without fear or strife

At Trails End we'll find all the good cowboy heroes
At Trails End we'll find our western lands as they once were
At Trails End they'll be no need for deadly six-guns
or fences of bloody barbed wire, that's for sure

At Trails End we'll be met by our loving Creator
At Trails End they'll be no need for us to eat or sleep
At Trails End we'll meet all of our lost loved ones
and be rewarded for all of our saved, lost sheep

At Trails End we'll live among Heaven's many rainbows
At Trails End we'll ride fast horses that never tire
At Trails End we'll get to meet our guardian angel
who protected us from hell's all-consuming fire

So, at our Trails End lies the promised land of milk and honey
At our end stands the doorway to eternal life
At our end grows the sweet grasses of Heaven
and its endless days without fear or strife

MONTANA'S SONG

Now, Montana's Song is an endless song
It's as endless as its majestic western sky
For its whole land daily sings of its given beauty
and now the only place left where fresh footprints of visiting angels lie

Its mountains sing of their liquid, cold streams
that keep its living valleys green far, far below
These mountains, the footstool of our designer God
who daily watches Montana's ongoing and never-ending show

There's the drumming sound of its thundering buffalo
and the piercing cry of high-flying eagle screams
There's the summer music of its tiny hummingbirds
whose speedy wings stir the thoughts of our own human dreams

There are whitetail deer and antelope and honey-seeking bears
each richly adding to Montana's never ceasing song
And birds and fish in uncountable living numbers
who add their own living melodies each day long

There are winter's sounds within its falling soft snows
and leaving impressions of a hunting owl's feathered wings
And the ever-present wild coyote track
who lifts its nightly voice to our universe and sings

There are singing bull frogs in their warm ponds of August
and pine singing winds in each passing summer storm
There's the heard crackling sounds of its blazing sunsets
that keeps our own singing hearts peaceful and warm

There are cougar and elk and the returning wolf
each plays their special part in Heaven's laid plans
For every living thing in Montana has their own part to play
each singing under the guidance of their Maker's hands

For Montana's Song is an endless song
It is as endless as its majestic western sky
For its whole land daily sings of its given beauty
and now the only place left where fresh footprints of visiting angels lie

OUR HALLELUJAH SONG

To sing hallelujah in the morning
To sing hallelujah all day long
I sing hallelujah within my soul now
For my heart carries Heaven's redemption song

It sings the story of Jesus
It sings the story of His cross
It sings the story of His forgiving grace
It sings of eternal life, not of the fires of hell or loss

It sings of the coming rewards for His own sheep
It sings the compelling story of His life
It sings the story of His spilled blood, my friend
It sings to my own children and my loving wife

For we now sing hallelujah every morning
We now sing hallelujah all day long
We sing hallelujah within our souls everyday now
For our hearts now carry Heaven's redemption song

THIS MONTANA LIVIN'

I love hunting deer in Montana's purple sage brush
I love wearing a cowboy hat and driving a pickup with guns
I love fishing in trout-filled crystal rivers
I love This Montana Livin' and its four seasons of western fun

Of crowded cities it's still plum empty
There's still endless room to catch one's breath
A land of eagle-filled skies it is
A place to learn the value of one's life before death

All outdoor dreams it's known to answer
It's just a foretaste of Heaven's values to come
A place of rugged shining snowy mountains
That each evening in blazing glory devours its setting sun

For I love hunting deer in Montana's purple sage brush
I love wearing a cowboy hat and driving a pickup with guns
I love fishing in trout-filled crystal rivers
I love This Montana Livin' and its four seasons of western fun

EDEN BRIGHT

Oh Montana, my Montana
designed by God for my soul's delight
Oh Montana, my Montana
land of endless sky, still so clear and Eden Bright

You've answered all my needed dreams
and fed my starving human heart
You've cured my selfish human eyes
and taught me to be wilderness smart

You've allowed me to see the gateway of Heaven
within the colors of your rainbows, born of soft western light
You've allowed me to hear the distant songs of angels
descending from your uncountable stars each and every night

You've taught me the true meaning of God's given love
That to all others I should daily give
For you truly are the last best place
and to no other place should I ever again desire to live

Oh Montana, my Montana
designed by God for my soul's delight
Oh Montana, my Montana
land of endless sky, still so clear and Eden Bright

THIS LOVE BORN
THE WEDDING POEM

Now there are many things I think
we shall never live to see
But that does not really matter, my love
For This Love Born is our life's future key

To grow old together, to live a productive life
To share our coming moments as husband and wife
To laugh and cry, to comfort our shared sorrows and pains
To grow stronger in This Love Born is our treasure to gain

To take long walks in a summer's warm falling rain
To pick Heaven's wild flowers will be our memories to gain
There'll be those long, cold winters, and books we'll share
and those sick times when, for each other, we'll care

There'll be coming times when we'll be angry
and hurtful words at each other we'll exchange
But This Love Born will survive
because This Love Born will never change

There'll be new places to go and new things to do
as we share our lives together under God's skies of angel-blue
And when we're old, This Love Born will still be just as strong
For in all our coming years we'll have sung love's lasting song

But then there will be many things I think
we shall never live to see
But that no longer really matters now, my love
for today is the day I marry thee

NO THING SO BEAUTIFUL

No Thing So Beautiful
as Montana's wilderness embrace
No Thing So Beautiful
as her winter snows of cold crystal lace

No Thing So Beautiful
as her vast western lands
No Thing So Beautiful
as seeing the work here of God's loving hands

No Thing So Beautiful
as her towering trees that toward Heaven reach
No Thing So Beautiful
as to what her many gifts to our souls teach

No Thing So Beautiful
as her mighty blue sky
No Thing So Beautiful
as the joy of seeing her wild eagles fly

For nothing is so beautiful
as Montana's wilderness embrace
Nothing so beautiful, my friend
as her winter snows of cold crystal lace

RAINBOW BEAUTIFUL

Rainbow Beautiful
shining within my eyes
Rainbow Beautiful
born from angry Montana summer skies

Rainbow Beautiful
God's promise never to flood the earth again
Rainbow Beautiful
singing within the falling rain and stormy winds

Rainbow Beautiful
you're a treasure to these western lands
Rainbow Beautiful
painted by God's loving and caring hands

Rainbow Beautiful
your colors my heart has healed and freed
Rainbow Beautiful
touching every rock and living Montana tree

Rainbow Beautiful
softly upon every eagle's feathered wings
Rainbow Beautiful
more value than all of mankind's gold and treasured things

So, Rainbow Beautiful
now shining within my human eyes
Oh, Rainbow Beautiful
born this day from angry Montana summer skies

CRYSTAL BRIGHT

In the valley of the Bitterroot Mountains
on a warm and soft summer's night
If you stand really, really still
you'll hear all of Heaven's stars blink Crystal Bright

You'll hear the diving wings of a hunting nighthawk
and hear wild Montana deer eating the new grass of summer green
You'll hear the final cry of falling meteors
as across its darkened skies their dying good-byes they scream

You'll hear the mating music of grasshoppers
echoing throughout its late-night cooling air
You'll then discover just how much its worth
to be living in this Bitterroot Valley that's so beautiful and rare

You'll hear the tiny sounds of hungry field mice
as they run about seeking seeds for next winter's coming snow
You'll hear the deep calls of giant bullfrogs
as they bask in the light of a Bitterroot moon all aglow

You'll hear splashing sounds of feeding brown trout
as they jump in pure waters of melted, high mountain ice
You'll never want to leave this Bitterroot Valley ever again
for it's magic your soul and heart will capture and entice

For in my valley of the Bitterroot Mountains
on a warm and soft summer's night
I've stood really, really still
and heard all of Heaven's stars blink Crystal Bright

MY MONTANA

Oh Montana, My Montana
Birth-land of the wild eagle's cry
Oh Montana, My Montana
Beautiful land of snowy mountains high

You're blessed by the touch of Heaven
Your lakes are full of crystal waters pure
Your vastness is so overwhelming
Your many gifts my soul did cure

Your skies flow a deep ocean-blue
Your valleys lie soft and summer-green
Your rivers under all rainbows born
Your gentle spirit taught my heart how to dream

Your springs are full of scented flowers
Your summers lie under the blazing western sun
Your falls are painted of ever-changing colors
Your winters lie white where the wild wolf runs

You're blessed by the touch of Heaven
Your lakes are full of crystal waters pure
Your vastness is so overwhelming
Your many gifts my soul did cure

Oh Montana, My Montana
Birth-land of the wild eagle's cry
Oh Montana, My Montana
Beautiful land of snowy mountains high

GOD KNOWS

Where does our soul go
when our body dies?
What happens to our memories
when in final stillness we lie?

Where do our Montana eagles go
when they take their last breath?
What happens to them
when they fall to the earth after their death?

Why is our world
the only place where human life grows?
Why not the other planets
out where the solar wind blows?

Why do little babies die
before they have their chance to live?
How did God make woman
out of Adam's sleeping rib?

For God knows where our soul goes
when our body dies
He Knows what happens to all our
memories when in final stillness we lie

He Knows where all Montana eagles go
when they take their last flying breath,
He knows each one by name
when they fall to the earth after their death

He Knows why our earth
is the only place where human life grows
He knows why the other planets lie lifeless
out where His solar wind blows.

He Knows why little babies die
before they have their chance to live,
He knows how He made
woman out of Adam's sleeping rib

For only God Knows
all the answers to all known things
That's why He's God, our Creator
and the maker of eagles everywhere with soaring wings

OUR AMERICAN WEST

In this land of endless dreams
there runs liquid-ice, pure water streams
There are vast mountain ranges, topped with angel-white snow
and its skies are of the bluest found of this my heart knows

There's no other land quite like it, no matter where you look
It's far more beautiful than any pictures found in any book
It's rugged and wild and its air is of the earth's very best
It's all the lands still found in Our American West

Its history is rich and from it many lessons have come
Some still bear their scars, passed on from father to son
For it once stood before the heavens, fenceless and free
It was at one time a land full of standing virgin trees

There were no great cities then built by the hand of man
There were only scattered Indian villages across its lands
The only thing the wind carried was the purest of air
Its land was then full of wild animals and the grizzly bear

Now, that time in history is long-ago lost
That first west is gone forever at a terribly high cost
But the second west still shines, it's still Heaven-blessed
It's all the lands still found in Our American West

For it's still the land of endless dreams
It's still full of liquid-ice pure water streams
There are vast mountain ranges topped with angel white snow
Its sky is still the bluest found of this my heart knows

There's no other land quite like it no matter where you look
It's far more beautiful than any pictures found in any book
It's rugged and wild and its air is of earth's very best
It's all the lands still found in Our American West

LIFE FORCE

In the high mountains of a Montana mid-winter's day
the deepest snows of its cold season lay
They lay awaiting next spring's returning warm sun
When they will melt and toward its mighty rivers run

For the snow is the Life Force to this dry, Montana land
It greens up the brown winter valleys and dry thirsty sand
It adds the color to each seen rainbow that fills its sky
It returns as rain in storm clouds as dark as midnight high

They sing to the deep sleeping flowers of next year's spring
These snows of Montana's winters the north winds bring
They hide all the scars from modern man's ever hungry deeds
They even hide the pheasant from the hawk in snow bent weeds

They cover the high mountains, the skier's downhill run
They cover Montana's landscape for its children to have fun
They give us the time to pause and reflect by a warming fire
They give us endless memories to fill our every winter's desire

For in the high mountains of a Montana mid-winter's day
the deepest snows of its cold season lay
They lay awaiting next spring's returning warm sun
When they will melt once again and toward its mighty rivers run

HEART OF GLASS

Why do I have a Heart Of Glass
so easily broken, so easily smashed?
What will it take to fix it
to make it stronger, to make it last?

Who has the gentle touch
I now need so bad?
Who has the wisdom to restore it
from the chilling grip of sad?

The darkness seems to engulf it
as I type and think and sit
My eyes so easily weep
that my escape now is to seek the dreams of sleep

High mountain beauty surrounds me
My soul feeds off its pine-scented breath
Yet my human heart only seems to hear
the approaching footsteps of death

So why was I born with a Heart Of Glass
so easily broken, so easily smashed?
Who is the One to fix it; who will make it stronger?
God is the One to make it last.

ALMOST A COWBOY

I once was Almost A Cowboy
when I was just a little snip of a kid
From every corner of the wild west
all the bad guys I planned to hang, or if needed, bullet-rid

I planned to rope every wild cow
that walked without a scaring brand
To catch me a real bronco bucking horse
somewhere out in its dry desert endless sand

Then learn how to ride it
no matter what its wildness did
Then learn how to be faster on the draw
than someone like Billy The Kid

I wanted to be the greatest cowboy
that was ever western-born
Upon my then youthful and uncluttered heart
and yet my unseen future I once had sworn

But later many things happened to change my course
and from my youthful cowboy dreams I was to finally stray
You see my first dreams never happened
for other paths my learning heart was to later obey

Now I'm on the down side
of life's high and slippery hill
My hair is gray; I've got bad knees
and it takes lots to keep me going; doctors and pills

But I'll always fondly remember
that when I was just a little snip of a kid
I was once Almost A Cowboy
who planned to hang all the bad guys or if needed back then, bullet-rid

THE LAST REAL COWBOY PLACE

I once saw an old Montana cowboy cry
and went over to console him, to ask him why.
"Well son," he said, "it's a long story, that's for sure
You see, I just lost my best friend and it's been hard to endure

"I just lost my partner of well over sixty years
We shared the hard times, the good times and many shed tears
We'd been through the thick and thin of this old life
You see I just lost my best friend, my lover, my beautiful wife

"But not all is lost in the sadness of her death
for what she left behind is found on my own living breath
For she wasn't afraid of dying since God she'd found
You see, she knew we'd be together again someday on Heaven's perfect ground

"Now see, son, she was blessed to have been a real cowboy's wife
for she daily breathed in the freshest air all her given life
Air so completely fresh it still carries Heaven's personal grace
and now to be found only here in Montana, The Last Real Cowboy Place

"She raised up our three children and their children too
and made sure everyone's school shoes were always brand new
Why she made more kinds of cookies than anyone ever before
and always had the welcome mat out at our ranch's front door

"She helped me herd and brand cattle with deep western pride
She cooked each meal and could break any horse so she could saddle-ride
She helped me fix fences and put up our needed winter hay
She worked from dawn to dusk every single-lived western day

"She fixed many a broken bone and a few snake bites too
She made most of our kids' clothes, looking store-bought new
She was a real whiz at fixin' almost any broken thing
She was found in church on Sundays where to God she'd pray
and in her angel voice sing

"But now she's gone and I miss her bad
Her saddle's cold and empty and my soul's more than sad
I miss her sweet voice and the smell of her auburn soft hair
My heart's bad broken son and in need of her gentle repair."

Well I told that old Montana cowboy, how sorry I was;
for his loss was truly deep
Then I had to turn and walk away so he wouldn't see me begin
to shake and weep
For I cried for his broken heart and the love he'd once had
as I walked back over to my wife,
Kissed her and told her why I was crying and so very sad

So now that I've told his story from a long-time ago
He'd be riding with her now under spring skies all aglow
I only hope that our paths will cross once again, someday
Up there in Heaven where all the good cowboy couples go
To rest, ride a lot and in its fenceless green pastures play

MY HOME SWEET HOME

Have you ever dreamed
of having a Montana rainbow touch your hand?
Or of seeing the battle ground
where Custer fought his last and tragic stand?

Have you ever dreamed of finding a Montana sapphire
while walking in its purple sage brush of remembered worth?
Or of someday feeding your heart an evening's warmth
of one of its blazing sunsets giving birth?

Have you ever dreamed
of living beneath a bright Montana-blue sky?
Or of hearing, in an early morning's summer mist,
one of its wild eagles fly by?

Have you ever dreamed
of seeing a Montana Indian dance and spirit-drum sing?
Or of wanting to rest and lie
in a high mountain meadow full of its wild flowers of spring?

Have you ever dreamed
of skiing on top of a Montana pine, buried twenty feet down?
Or of getting really close to one of its wild mule deer
by sneaking along its rocky and dusty dry, western ground?

Have you ever dreamed
of floating on a rushing Montana river on a hot summer night?
Or of trying to count its many different birds
whose songs will fill your soul with Montana's wild delight?

Have you ever dreamed
of casting a favorite dry fly on a windy Montana fall day?
Or of hunting one of its mighty bull elk
when its sky is full of snow and painted a cold November gray?

Have you ever dreamed
of camping under one of Montana's ancient giant pines?
Or of drinking some fire-brewed, steaming mountain coffee
when its weather is full of cold and snowy winter signs?

Have you ever dreamed
of seeing a great owl fly across one of its full fall moons?
Or of hearing a coyote's distant call
echoing in the river valley where the Bitterroot flower blooms?

Have you ever dreamed
of coming here where one can still breathe and roam?
For I once dreamed the very same dreams a long-time ago
and now I call Montana My Home Sweet Home

MONTANA
"THIS NOBLE LAND"

In This Noble Land, of silver sagebrush and scented pine
You'll find deer and antelope and expanding wolf-track sign
Its shining rivers travel mighty, icy cold and western free
This Noble Land is endless and wild and most pleasing to see

It's known for its big sky of sunny daily blue
and far more, than just another place to quickly pass through
For it still holds within itself the touch of Heaven's hand
It's God's finest work; for all children born, woman and man

It's full of cowboys and Indians and folks like you and me
and mighty snowy mountains most everywhere to see
You'll find elk and bears and coyotes that love to run
and breathless remembered sunsets in each setting sun

Now there's a beautiful kind of kindness in its people to find
Living proof of their awareness of God's grace and loving sign
Why they'll even give you the shirt off their hard-working back
Their compassion's real, each heart empty of "city blues black"

They're really very different, brave-hearted and pioneer-strong
For each carries within their souls Montana's birthing song
A song of its history so rich and western deep
The story of its joys, its losses, that will make you weep

For in This Noble Land of silver sage brush and scented pine
You'll find deer and antelope and expanding wolf-track sign
Its shining rivers travel mighty, icy cold and western free
This Noble Land is endless and wild and still the most pleasing
for of all of America to see

ANOTHER COWBOY
LIKE ME

Lord, when I die
and find myself Heaven-bound
When I get there, Lord
will I find Another Cowboy Like Me hanging around?

Will he still be wearing his favorite cowboy hat?
Will it be as soiled and beat up as mine?
Will his boots be scuffed and western-worn
and showing the effects of weather and time?

Will I have daily branding chores to do
on Your cattle upon Your ten thousand hills?
Will my new life with You, Lord,
be full of fresh wild horse rodeo-riding thrills?

Now I know I won't be packing no gun, Lord
For I've heard about the sign posted above Your golden gate
You know the one that says "NO GUNS ALLOWED IN HERE
FOR THIS PLACE IS PLUM EMPTY OF JEALOUSY AND HATE"

So, Lord, when I someday die
and find myself Heaven-bound
I just wanted to know when I get there, Lord
Will I find Another Cowboy Like Me hanging around?

THIS OLD COWBOY HAT

Now I've got This Old Cowboy Hat
It looks a hundred years old and as if chewed some by a packrat
I've worn it nearly every day for some forty years and more
Times when I was paycheck-weekend-rich and Monday-morning-poor

It's served me well, all these many working cowboy years
Through times of deep laughter and times of sad, graveyard tears
It's kinda my favorite; my good luck cowboy charm
In summer it saved my brains and kept me from winter's bitter harm

I've often used it as a thin sleeping pillow
on many a cold, cattle driving, high-plains night
I've even filled it up with canteen water
to give my horse a cooling drink in a hot summer's August light

Now I wouldn't trade it for nothin'
not even for a new 20-dollar gold piece, all shiny and fine
For it's my best and most trusted friend—it is
It has proved itself here in Montana's seasons of every kind

Why, I even remember putting a bunch of baby birds in it once
that had fallen out of their storm damaged nest
And then later on when I checked to see how they were doing
I can still remember my shock of finding their baby bird mess

I even got a bullet hole in it one day
from a long ago Saturday morning fight
One of the few times in my long, cowboy life
that my heart felt some real hard-time, fright

It was over a young red-headed Irish beauty
The new school teacher for our then small, but growing town
Who some drunken drifter had offended that day
that I left broken and bleeding on its western dusty ground

Now my hat has seen a lifetime of my cowboy ups and cowboy downs
It's heard a lifetime of my cowboy livin' working sounds
My times of being weekend-rich and Monday-morning-poor
My times in Sunday church and times when I got mad and swore

And someday, when the good Lord calls down for me
to mount up on His awaiting white horse and ride back home
You can count on me taking This Old Cowboy Hat of mine
and wearing it where the good old cowboys live to ride and roam

MONTANA DREAMER

Now some have called me a Montana Dreamer
because my soul is filled with the sounds of eagle cries
That my western heart is unlike most others
because I live for its each magic moment held prisoner
by its rugged, snow-capped, mountainous, crystal-blue sky

Some say my heart was long-ago seeded in the Garden of Eden
so my eyes could see the true depth of this land's given best
That I live only for those special moments of its seen splendor
That my soul somehow understands the value of its quiet rest

Some say I'm a different breed of Montana writer
That I love its deep winters and summers of all rainbows bold
That I'm down-to-earth open and honest and western friendly
That my heart was cast from an old type of cowboy mold

Some say I carry within, the vision of its coming tomorrows
That I'm one of the guardians for its lands in which I live
That I and others understand the richness of keeping its values
That to pass it on is the gift we've been commanded to give

So, some have called me a Montana Dreamer
because my soul is filled with the sounds of eagle cries
That my western heart is unlike most others
because I live for its each magic moment, held prisoner
by its rugged, snow-capped, mountainous, crystal-blue sky

DARE TO DREAM

Dare To Dream
of what you might someday be
Dare To Dream, young Montanan
for your western heart is your future key

Dare To Dream
of what gift you might someday give
Dare To Dream, young Montanan of
how your life you'll share and live

Dare To Dream
your dreams other lives might someday change
Dare to Dream, young Montanan
let your dreams all this world taste and change

Dare To Dream
remember from where your dreams first came
Dare To Dream, young Montanan
keep love foremost in your life's coming game

So, Dare To Dream young Montanan
of what you might someday be
Dare To Dream, always
for your western heart is your future key

DREAMLAND

In Dreamland all little cowboys sing and yodel, too
They ride white horses under skies of high-mountain blue
Their hearts are pure; they wear fancy, fast-draw guns
They're brave and tough and from the bad guys they never run

They always win and never ever seem to bleed or die
They love their horses and know how to, real kindness, apply
They break every girl's heart; from marriage they always flee
They never cuss, only say, "yes m'am, no sir and golly gee"

They never drink hard whiskey, chew, or smoke
They always have spending money and never seem sad or broke
They never run out of bullets and they never ever miss
They laugh a lot and all the pretty ranch girls hug and kiss

They can go for many days without food or fresh water to drink
They're real smart and wise and know how to deep down think
Their boots are always clean, they never need a shave
They can out ride a lightning bolt and know how to behave

For I once lived that Dreamland where I could sing and yodel, too
I had my white horse to ride under skies of high mountain blue
My heart was then pure; I always wore a fancy fast-draw gun and
from its bad guys I never was known to flinch or run

But now I'm old and somewhat gray
and my childhood Dreamland was lost in my growing up ways,
But I can still remember with a smile, those days of long-ago
Dreams of cowboys and high western mountains and sunsets
so rich and forever within my soul, still aglow

THE APOCALYPSE OF THE YELLOWSTONE HERD

My soul heard their dying cry
In fields of snowy-blood my heart saw them lie
Each done in by the madness and stupidity of heartless men
This inhumane and savage slaughter they can't defend

Nearly two-thirds of its bison the winter and man did kill
The sounds of their gun-fire still echo from each mountain,
valley and sagebrush hill
They cut off their heads with eyes so lifeless, sad and gray
To be bought by more heartless men some future auction day

Once they were the greatest herd of animals ever to roam
the face of our now shrinking earth
Numbering some 60 million, before our forefathers nearly
exterminated them for their hides and tongues of golden worth
Something has gone very wrong within the minds of modern men
that still allowed them to die in such an inhumane way
Have we learned nothing from our past sins from that long-ago day?

For my heart shall forever weep for each bison that had to die
Those that died in the fields and hills of snowy-blood
I shall forever see them in remembered sadness lie
Each allowed to perish by the weak minds of heartless men who to God, someday, will
have to answer for this shameful act when their own sad lives here finally end

WOLF DREAMS

Have you ever wondered just what a wild wolf dreams about
when it sleeps beneath our western stars on a cold winter's night?
Does it dream only now of the angry and fearful face of man
who also dreams of seeing it in their rifle's telescopic sight?

Or does it still dream of its once endless and quiet lands
of long before the devouring breath of mankind was born?
Or might it be dreaming of the warmth of last summer's sun
not to be felt again for many a coming cold winter's morn'

Might it be dreaming of yesterday's killing of a barren deer
who ran from it until it finally collapsed in breathless fear?
Or might it be dreaming of the cool taste of a pure water stream
while listening to the dying spirit of our wilderness scream

So, have you ever wondered just what a wild wolf dreams about
when it sleeps beneath our western stars on a cold winter's night?
Does it dream only now of the angry and fearful face of man
who also dreams of seeing it in their rifle's telescopic sight?

THE BLUE BIRD SONG

The Blue Bird Song
is what the western blue bird sings
The beautiful color of Montana's sky, it is
and the favorite of Heaven's reigning King

MY MONTANA REMEMBERED

Of golden sunsets and mighty mountains high
My Montana Remembered is where my ashes will someday lie
They'll lie within its vastness, becoming part of its eternal breath
joined as one someday when I lie in final death

For it's given me the understanding to see the heavens high
It's given me the insight to feel its spirit's gentle cry
It's guided me into its past to hear its first eagle screams
It's allowed my soul to dream all of its past Indian dreams

It speaks to me within its windy, pine-scented, western air
and taught me to be brave, to question, to dare
It's showed me the softness and its snows of angel white
It's changed my heart forever and taught my soul how to write

It's given me many visions of how I should daily live
and showed me God's love to all others I must give
It speaks to me in its every sunrise, its every sunset too
It talks to all who live under its skies of sunny western blue

So, of golden sunsets and mighty mountains high
My Montana Remembered is where my ashes will someday lie
They'll lie within its vastness, becoming part of its eternal breath
joined as one someday when I lie in final death

THIS HEALING LAND

It's here in Montana within This Healing Land
where I've found the creative touch of God's artistic hand
I've found all its many rainbows shining and painted bright
I've found its every sunset full of life-changing light

I've seen its speedy antelope, its wolf, its bear
For this healing Montana land is soul-easy and kind and rare
I've found that its high mountains hold up its deep blue sky
I've seen its bald eagles and heard their haunting freedom cry

I've heard its Indians and their chanting songs sung slow
and seen within their eyes their ancient fires of long ago
I discovered my soul's hunger for its here it learned to feed
and my heart is fulfilled it met every human need

It's changed me forever in the twinkling of an eye
It filled all my being with its crystal-living sky
And should I ever leave here, no matter where I might go
everyone will see in my eyes this land's healing glow

For it's here in Montana within This Healing Land
where I've found the creative touch of God's artistic hand
I've found all its many rainbows shining and painted bright
I've found its every sunset full of life changing light

A COWBOY'S HEART

A Cowboy's Heart
is what I have to give
If you'll just come and bunk with me
and in marriage my dreams share and live

For I'll build you a Montana ranch house
made of hand-cut Ponderosa Pine
That will stand the test of eternity
as my heart's lovin' and caring sign

Then underneath clear skies painted endless western blue
we'll live out our lives together until they're someday through
Then we'll ride out in search of Heaven, holding lovin' hands
to seek out its green pastures within its promised lands

So, it's just A Cowboy's Heart
that's all I have to give
If you'll just come and bunk with me
and in marriage my dreams share and live

OUR PROMISED LANDS

At the far end of our own life's journey
lies the warmth of God's awaiting hands
Where we'll finally find our eternal peace
A place us cowboys call Our Promised Lands

Endless lands without wars or sickness
The blind will see, the lame will run and walk
Finally free from all of our earthly sorrows
Why even the deaf will hear and talk

Endless lands void of all meanness and anger
No color of skin will any of us see
For we'll have been finally released
from the dark sin of human jealousy

For at the far end of our own life's journey
lies the warmth of God's awaiting hands
Where we'll finally find our eternal peace
A place us cowboys call Our Promised Lands

MONTANA'S WAY

I hear human voices in ever growing numbers
talking of heading Montana's Way
And I fear deep within my listening soul
each will be bringing with them the shadows of their own decay

For you see, this is where it all began
so many billions of dreams ago
When God Himself first started out right here
when He made all the things we've learned to love and know

But I now hear human voices, in ever growing numbers
talking of heading Montana's Way
And I fear deep within my listening soul
each will be bringing with them the shadows of their own decay

MONTANA IN TIME

They say her sky still runs blue near forever
That there's still room left for one to breathe and dream
That her ageless mountains still stand free and strong
and their melting snows still feed her endless flowing, crystal streams

For Montana In Time
still bears the mighty soul of long, long ago
When her first-born lived within her harmony true
for they were then a proud people, of this I've come to know

For they then loved and cared for her and knew her well
long before the white man came and brought along his own personal hell
Long before they learned of the man's soul's sadness and searing pain
for what the white man brought her first-born, gave them nothing to gain

Now her first-born have all been pushed aside
no longer to freely roam within her, or the buffalo to hunt for meat and hide
For Montana In Time has since changed in many, many ways
yet still the same of old, if you dare dream, the dream of her bygone days

So, some still say her sky runs blue near forever
and that there's still room left for one to breathe and dream
But it's my heart that can't seem to forget her first-born
whose countless tears still run deep within her endless flowing, crystal streams

LITTLE COWBOYS

Now Little Cowboys they never cry
for with cap gun in hand each is ready to fight and die
They'll fight a cattle rustler, or even a wild hungry bear
but will never kiss a cowgirl not even on a two-bit dare

For Little Cowboys are tough little men
and within their dreams, all goodness they'll fight to defend
They'll play the role of sheriff and ride a wild wooden horse
but will never play with dolls that's just too silly of course

They pack their paper saddle bags full of sweet jelly beans
then explore the back yard within their daily cowboy dreams
To be a great western hero to put the guys away
until its nap time when their dreams must await another day

So Little Cowboys now they never cry
for with cap gun in hand each is ready to fight and die
They'll fight a cattle rustler, or even a wild hungry bear
but will never ever kiss a cowgirl not even on a two-bit dare

SINGING STREAMS

Within my nightly Montana dreams
I often hear the gentle songs of its crystal streams
Their soft singing voices fill my thirsty listening soul
Their living words, to my heart, endless old stories have told

Stories from long before the first white man
when this western land was still free, open and pure
Stories of its first born, the Indians
who long ago learned, this western land to love and endure

Stories of its uncountable wild animals
more than all Africa, has ever known
Stories of their beautiful living value
long before the evil seeds of powder were sown

Stories of its first stillness
when only the wind's young voice, was heard
Stories from its first given day
eons before the birth of the first human word

Stories of great eternal meaning
then seen and heard by the blowing winds of Creation's time
Its first stories still carried in the hearts of angels
who still fly above this special land, gentle and kind

For within my nightly Montana dreams
I often hear the gentle songs of its crystal streams
Their soft singing voices fill my thirsty listening soul
Their living words, to my heart, endless old stories have told

THE LAST MONTANA COWBOY

The Last Montana Cowboy died last night
Into the setting western sun he quietly rode away
Bypassing that other well-known place
Upward to Heaven he rode to give his horse some fresh hay

And when he arrived before Heaven's golden gate
St. Peter asked him his name
"Why I'm The Last Cowboy from Montana," he said,
"Glad to meet you, St. Peter, just the same."

"Well, welcome son," St. Peter said,
"Why have you come this way?"
"I've come because there's no room left in Montana to roam
or any quiet place left there for me to stay."

"You see, St. Peter, Montana used to be vast and open
One could ride there endlessly and follow their dreams
But now the land is growing full of hateful people
with so much sadness within their hearts it seems."

"So, I've come here to Heaven, to find some peace
To ride each day, once or twice at least
I'm seeking fresh, sweet grass and clear waters too
Why, St. Peter, I want to ride all eternity through."

For it was just last night when The Last Montana Cowboy died
Into the setting western sun he quietly rode away
Bypassing that well-known other place
Upward to Heaven he rode to give his horse some fresh hay

MONTANA STARS

Montana Stars nightly displayed in crystal western skies
Every star is soul food for each star-gazing Montanan's eyes
Their stars are always blazing, far above their Eden lands
For every star was designed for just them by their Creator's star-maker hands

MONTANA ON MY MIND

I've got Montana On My Mind all the time now
ever since her western beauty took captive my soul
For her forever, cowboy-colored big skies
have taught me what it really means to be alive and bold

She speaks to me through her boldness, her wide vastness
and her trout streams that rush wild and hard winter cold
For I've found the value of her singing mountains
to be worth far more to me than all of mankind's foolish gold

For her living lands are truly wilderness special
for its only here where real angels can be clearly seen
For their songs daily echo from her snow-capped mountains
whose jagged peaks touch this land of Heaven's best dreams

Her winters are of lasting cold and deep-powder snow
Her springs smell of God's wild flowers in remembered bloom
Her dry summers birth forth smoke jumpers and forest fires
While her fall always bears the western hunter's savage moon

So, I've got Montana On My Mind all the time now
ever since her western beauty took captive my soul
For her forever cowboy-colored big skies
have taught me what it really means to be alive and bold

THEIR TRAIL OF ENDLESS TEARS

On wild painted horses
the Indians once ruled all this Montana land
They lived proud within its then unspoiled vastness
Each then guided by the Great Spirit's hand

With simple but deadly handmade weapons
they lived free for many thousands of years
Until the coming of the white man
who introduced to them Their Trail Of Endless Tears

For the white man took all that they had
He took until there was nothing left to give
He all but stole from these once proud people
their very will to breathe and in freedom live

So, by the thousands they vanished
from all these lands in which we now live
Yet their rich history and great knowledge
still has much wisdom to offer and give

For they once knew these lands, as we'll never know
and gave thanks for all things the Great Spirit did grow
From the buffalo to the deer and endless fish-filled streams
to the many eagles that gave them their journey dreams

So, with simple but deadly handmade weapons
they lived free, for many thousands of years
Until the coming of the white man
who then introduced to them Their Trail Of Endless Tears

RAINBOW'S END

Hey dreamer, your Rainbow's End lies where the west winds lie
It's an awaiting paradise, full of fresh blue, Montana skies
It's overflowing with tall mountains and clear water streams
It's the American birthland of wilderness and wild eagle screams

Its great western rivers run snowy cold, fresh, pure and clean
It's where wind songs are heard in every towering pine seen
Where winter's breath lets its wild flowers sleep and dream
It's a land of lasting fullness; its far more than it seems

So, look westward dreamer and you'll see your Rainbow's End
It's awaiting you just around your next dream's bend
It's overflowing with tall mountains and clear water streams
It's called Montana, the American birthland of wilderness
and wild eagle screams

THE LAND OF FREEDOM

Oh, Montana
Oh, mighty land of blazing summer sun
Oh, land of majestic snowy mountains
Oh, land of my western freedom and carried six-gun

Oh, land of grazing buffalo
Oh, land of the mighty grizzly bear
Oh, land of cowboys and Indians
Oh, land of big skies, so blue and fair

Oh, land of many deer
Oh, land of rushing pure streams
Oh, land of God's given best
Oh, land of rare beauty and found human dreams

Oh, land of wild bucking horses
Oh, land of tumbling weeds and singing pine
Oh, land of racing rainbows
Oh, land of rare stillness, so gentle, so kind

Oh, land of wind-swept prairie
Oh, land of the branded cow's cry
Oh, land of lightning and wild fires
Oh, land of smoke-jumpers who sometimes die

Oh, land of rugged people
Oh, land of Custer's final cry
Oh, land of remembered sunsets
Oh, land of eagle-filled skies

Oh, Montana
Oh, mighty land of blazing summer sun
Oh, land of majestic snowy mountains
Oh, land of my western freedom-carried six-gun

MONTANA REASONS

There are no stars quite so bright
as all the stars seen in a Montana's summer's night
There's no air still so pure
as its fresh mountain air your soul will cure

There's no other land so beautiful or nice
where pristine waters still taste as cold as pure liquid ice
There's no other western sky so full of wild eagle screams
or any other place that can fulfill all your heart's own dreams

For there's no need here for the thoughts of worldly things
like fancy big city clothes or shiny diamond, golden rings
There's no rhyme or reason for one to ever again rush or speed
For here you'll learn to relax and good books, winter-time read

You see, there's a brand new you just waiting to be reborn
It'll happen your very first-tasted fresh Montana morn'
You'll hear the hunting beats from a hawk's seeking wings
You'll hear its wilderness spirit, that first morning sing

For you see, there are no stars quite so bright
as all the stars seen in a Montana's, summer's night
There's no air still so pure
as its fresh mountain air your soul will cure

WHERE ALL COWBOYS COME TO DREAM

In this western land of many snowy mountains
In this place Where All Cowboys Come To Dream
You'll find the heart-land of the west's very soul
You'll find the birth-place of all clear water streams

You'll find the handy work of our designer God
in every place you might choose to look to one's spirit
And what you'll find is far more breath-taking
than any taken picture in any fancy printed book

In the spring all its lands lie awash in wildflowers
Their rainbow colors will hand to one's spirit Heaven's key
In the fall it's the echoing mountain call of the bull elk that
opens the door to our heart to let our blind eyes see

In the summer, it's the vast herds of hungry range cattle
that feed off its land warmed by its magic spell, "season of the sun"
In the winter the magic spell cast from its snowy voice
that calls all skiers to its high mountains to have downhill fun

For in this western land of many snowy mountains
In this place Where All Cowboys Come to Dream
You'll still find the heart-land of the west's very soul
You'll still find the birth-place of every Montana, clear water stream

OF WHAT VALUE

Of What Value is just one Montana eagle really worth?
Of What Value is it to all of us who share this earth?
Of What Value for our souls, to hear its pure wild cry?
Of What Value for both of us to have breathable skies?

Of What Value for our shared waters to be safe and clean?
Of What Value for our future, for our children to dream?
Of What Value to all other living things under our sky?
Of What Value are our oceans where most of our oxygen lies?

So, Of What Value is just one Montana eagle really worth?
Of What Value is it to all of us, who share this earth?
Of What Value for our souls to hear its pure wild cry?
Of What Value to all of us to have breathable, clean skies?

IN THE EYES OF THE EAGLE

In The Eyes Of The Eagle
you'll see the free spirit of the west's open skies
You'll see within them its many mountains, its crystal rivers
A land where the lost dreams of many brave men still lie

In the cry of the eagle
you'll hear the real soul of the wilderness scream
You'll hear the many voices of all its wildlife saying,
that the eagle and you are as one if you let your heart freely dream

In the heart of the eagle
the very blood of Heaven runs hot and pure
It gives the eagle its strength, its endless will
to the mighty western winds, use and endure

In the breath of the eagle
the true rawness of all nature can be found
It gives the eagle its part to play
both in the air and on the earth's ground

In the feather of the eagle
the special work of God is easily seen
Its feathered beauty will never be forgotten
as it will live always, somewhere in all your living dreams

For it's In The Eyes Of The Eagle
where you'll find the free spirit of the west's open skies
You'll see within them its many mountains, its crystal rivers
A land where the lost dreams of many brave men still lie

THE TRAIL BOSS

Have you ever been
real-cowboy, saddle sore?
Have you ever had so much to drink
that you couldn't find the bunk house door?

Have you ever been stuck in an outhouse
without a single piece of paper in sight?
Have you ever gotten a black eye
in some western town barroom fight?

Have you ever fallen asleep in the saddle
while trying to keep some cattle calm on a stormy night?
Have you ever shot a rattler plum dead
as it tried real hard your leg to bite?

Have you ever got so crazy winter-cold
that you thought you and your horse were going to die?
Have you ever thought much about the life you live
underneath the west's vast blue skies?

Have you ever eaten red beans and salted pork
by a chuck wagon's warming fire's light?
Have you ever used your saddle as a pillow
while counting the stars of the heavens so distant bright?

Have you ever heard a coyote sing
to the rising moon on a hot August night?
Have you ever felt the inner peace of knowing
that the western life you live is real and cowboy-right?

Have you ever had to pull a new-coming calf
during a late winter's savage, calf-killing storm?
Have you ever lost a best friend during a cattle drive
and had to dig his grave in the early light of a sad new morn?

Have you ever had your heart broke by a gal
in some long-remembered trail-town saloon?
Have you ever had to put a favorite horse down
that left your heart full of sadness gloom?

Have you ever wondered just where old cowboys really go
when too tired and old to do their cowboy thing?
Why they just ride off to Heaven, didn't you know?
They report to The Trail Boss, cowboy songs for Him they'll sing

AVALANCHE
THIS WHITE RIVER OF DEATH

In the blink of a circling eagle's eye
This White River Of Death can kill and maim
when it roars down from its high mountain resting places
like a savage and deadly, uncaring runaway train

Hard crust on the top
soft crystallized powder underneath
the slightest sound can set it plunging
to bury the foolish and unknowing in its darkness of deep

Then to be trapped in a snowy world of an awaiting silent death
Little air to breathe if taken only in shallow, cold breath
held still by its weight; the weight of its crushing grip
Ever so slowly into the door of death most will quickly slip

Their tears will lie frozen and silent
until next spring's revealing warm breath
are all the unlucky, winter ones
who played and gambled below its roaring white death

So, in just a blink of a circling eagle's eye
This White River Of Death can kill and maim
when it roars down from its high mountain resting places
like a savage and deadly, uncaring runaway train

THE STILLNESS

In The Stillness of her quiet beauty
Of God's created best she stands all alone
This special place called Montana
From Heaven's finest seeds was sown

From her rolling and endless grass-covered plains
to her mighty snowy mountains high
She's blessed with the purest of waters
and a daily boldness of big western sky

She's a healer of hearts
and food for the ever-hungry, human soul
She's a shining gift of our Creator's love
Within her four seasons; in deep beauty she unfolds

Her trees touch the very foothills of Heaven
where angels sing, and wild eagles always fly
Her air is clean pine-scented fresh
where the colors of racing rainbows live and die

For Montana is the blessed of the blessed
of all the lands of this given earth
Blessed to be a place of such grandeur
Blessed to be a place of such deep spiritual worth

MY SHINING TIME

I miss those old days of sourdough bread and dried red beans
and the sound of salt bacon dancing on a buffalo chip fire
I miss that cold stillness of a rising Montana's winter's moon
that long-ago filled my then youthful cowboy desires

I miss my days of past foolishness, my days of lasting strength
Those long-ago days when any wild horse I could ride and break
Days of packing a six-gun, days of dry and dusty cattle drives
Days when I was a working cowboy, so young and so much alive

But these old bones of mine now they just sit and rest
Long past their working years long past their cowboy best
Long past My Shining Time that's now long faded away
These old bones of mine in a rocking chair now mostly stay

For I miss those days of sourdough bread and dried red beans
and the sound of salt bacon dancing on a buffalo chip fire
I miss that cold stillness of a rising Montana's winter's moon
that long-ago so filled my then-youthful cowboy desires

SKY PAINTER

There's a ranch somewhere in the west
called Rainbow's End so the angels of Heaven say
It's where the Sky Painter lives and works
who paints our western sunsets each evening's fading day

He paints no two ever the same
His deep love is seen throughout our day-ending skies
And sometimes He paints only in a soft crystal blue
that fills our human souls with wonderment and deep sighs

Now He paints the thoughts of His own perfect heart
no other painter can do the same
For He paints for us His own created children
to help ease our sometimes sorrows and pain

And when the full depth of our western winter finally comes,
He paints only in the shades of gray and snowy white
Then later, He'll start mixing new colors for our coming spring
When he'll again fill our western skies with His rainbow light

For there really is a western ranch called Rainbow's End
because the angels of Heaven cannot lie
It's where the Sky Painter lives and works
who paints our western sunsets in each evening's fading sky

THE MONTANA CABIN FEVER PRAYER

Lord, the deepness of this endless Montana winter
has taken a firm grip on this old cowboy's lonely mind
As I sit in this here snow-bound cabin
made of hand cut, old yellow, Montana mountain pine

You see the snow has been falling forever, Lord
from Your gray-ladend, snowy winter skies
And if it doesn't stop real soon, oh Lord
I think I'll soon lie down and close my eyes and die

For I've read every darn canned food label
in this shrinking cabin more than twice
Why Lord, the only friends I have to talk to
are a pair of small gray, mountain mice

Why Lord, it's only the first of January
and the hardest part is yet to come
In fact, oh Lord, it's been three weeks now
since I last saw Your shining sun

Now I know the only thing that keeps me going, Lord
is the endless beauty of this snow-bound Montana place
For its a land I call cowboy heaven
with few people and lots of open, breathable space

But oh Lord, the deepness of this endless Montana winter
has now taken a firm grip on this old cowboy's lonely mind
So how about sending spring kind of early this year, Lord as
Your cowboy lovin', caring-for-me sign

WILD FIRE

Wild Fire! Wild Fire!
To hear its blazing cry
Deep dryness; so little rain
To watch our west explode and die

Yellow shirts, Surrey bombers
Acid smoke and bloodshot eyes
Falling ashes from beauty lost
Each summer fills our west with gray hazy skies

Fleeing wildlife; destroyed human dreams
Consuming everything in its charging path
Wild Fire! Wild Fire!
The burning voice of hell's fiery wrath

OF EARTH, OF WIND, OF FIRE

I'm the American west, a mighty land
I'm Of Earth, Of Wind, Of Fire
I'm the land of majestic, snowy mountains majesty
I'm of a vastness that the human heart I still inspire

I bear roaring rivers, quiet lakes and endless flowing streams
My sky is big and blue and full of golden eagle screams
I'm the land of elk and deer and the fierce, grizzly bear
I once was touched by Heaven's hand; I'm of a beauty so rare

I still weep for the forgotten graves of the foolish, the bold
Dreamers each, who perished in my searing heat, my bitter cold
Their wagon scars I still show from their time of long ago
I'm the place where their dreams they tried to plant and grow

My people of today are hardworking and rugged and western wise
They're ranchers and cowboys and those who wear city ties
They're of different seen colors, from different far-away lands
They're my children all; each has left their mark upon my ageless and dry sands

For I'm the American west, a mighty land
I'm Of Earth, Of Wind, Of Fire
I'm the land of majestic, snowy mountains majesty
I'm of a vastness that the human heart I still inspire

MONTANA SUMMER

It's summertime again here in Montana
Where one can still live, proud and free
Where the mighty American eagle can still be found
in great numbers for all the rest of America to see

We're a people of a rugged sort
Hard-working with hearts of western gold
We deeply care about the land we live on
We're Montanans straight shooters and bold

We raise cattle, horses and lots of kids
We work hard on the lands on which we live
For we'd live no other place if given a chance
For no other place can Montana's deep beauty give

Now, Montana is God's favorite summer place
For it's where all of His rivers run, blue-ribbon best
For nowhere else will you ever find a place like it
For it's here where He comes each summer to fly-fish and rest

Our rugged mountains speak of many things
We're where great rivers catch a flowing western sky
For Montana holds the hearts of many kinds of people
whose souls know how to, its vastness of deep beauty apply

For It's summer time again here in my Montana
A place where I can still live proud and free
A place where the mighty American eagle can still be found
in great numbers for all the rest of America to see

THE SAGA OF THE JELLY BEAN COWBOY

He's known as The Jelly Bean Cowboy
He's barely but five years old
Always seen packing a fancy cap gun
and hard-riding his old stick horse, cowboy bold

His boots are well scuffed and dirty
His cowboy hat soiled and sandbox bent
He spends his every daylight hour in his backyard
playing in his great-grandfather's old cavalry army tent

His voice is the voice of many known cowboy heroes
He plays out his western dreams from dawn to dusk
The sounds from his fiery cap gun are daily heard
playing sheriff and riding his stick horse called old Cuss

His eyes are full of youthful mischief
They're the color of cold blue Winchester steel
His saddle bags always stuffed full of sweet jelly beans
They're his breakfast, his lunch and each dinner meal

Now there's none any faster with a gun, in his own mind's eye
He's been known to ride down and hog tie any dog found
He keeps his cap gun under his pillow when he sleeps
just in case he awakens to bad guy, gun-fire sounds

For he's known as The Jelly Bean Cowboy
He's barely but five years old
He's always seen packing a fancy cap-gun
and hard-riding his old stick horse, cowboy bold

MONTANA COWBOY BORN

I was born to be a Montana cowboy
I was born to be big city free
I was born to travel Montana's western lands
Born to brand all its wild cattle I see

I was born to pack a six-gun
I was born to answer to no man
I was born to be a rugged free spirit
Born to march to a different drummer's band

I was born for the smell of saddle leather
I was born for spurs and boots
I was born for fixing fences
Born to never wear no fancy, city suits

I was born to break wild bucking horses
I was born to eat my meals from an open fire
I was born to sleep below Montana's starry heavens
Born to fulfill my cowboy heart's every desire

For I was born to be a Montana cowboy
I was born to be big city free
I was born to travel Montana's western range
Born to brand all its wild cattle I see

MONTANA MEMORIES

I have many fond Montana Memories now
rooted deep within my human soul
For all these many years I've lived here
it has taught my heart how to live each day big-sky bold

Memories of a vastness, still so open, so deep, so western wide
Always so beautiful they make my heart sometimes cry
Memories of skies so pure and blue and each one angel-sent
Memories of her dancing rainbows so vivid and horseshoe bent

Memories of her mighty mountains
always full of wilderness winds and singing eagle screams
Memories of her spring melt-offs
that feeds and renews her many trout-filled, clear streams

Memories of her shaggy buffalo
and the thunder dust they cause when they run
Memories of her endless painted treasures
found within her each day's vivid setting sun

Memories of her deep winter snows
The life force of her every lake, river and stream
Memories of her first children, the Indians and the drum sounds,
from their first child's long ago spirit-story dreams

Memories of many good friends I've made here
and some to touch death I've lost along my traveled way
Memories of all the things I've learned since coming here
that tells me I'll see them all again on some future day

Memories of a distant calling to move my family west
that long-ago changed our hearts and souls in many, many ways
Those first memories still as fresh all these many years later
as they were when we came here that long ago, very first day

For I'm so blessed to have all these Montana Memories
Each one now and forever rooted deep within my human soul
For all these many years we've lived within her
she's still teaching us how to live each day big-sky bold

PALE MOON RIDER

Pale Moon Rider came a ridin'
with a shotgun in his preachin' hand
Spreading the word of the Gospel
throughout every part of the west's frontier lands

Now only fools laughed at him
all others knew better when he rode their way
For the Pale Moon Rider took care of everyone
who tried to stop his Gospel preachin' way

Now when some fool would try to stop him
from peacefully passing through
Why he'd just bow his head, pull his shotgun
and turn that fool, very, dead-blue

So, if you ever see him ridin' your way
with a shotgun in his preachin' hand
Don't be a fool and get in his way
unless you're ready to shake "the devil's hand"

MONTANA LAND

Below the stars, from God's given hand
lies my home, a place called Montana Land
A land of boundless beauty and ice-cold descending streams
cowboys and horses and remembered Indian dreams

There are eagles and antelope and high desert deer
and the mighty buffalo still seen in every Indian tear
Its land is so vast no poet can tell it all
where one's heart can still hear the wolf's distant call

There are grizzlies and black bears
and mountains that hold up crystal living skies
Wild endless rivers, high summer lakes
and hungry trout that await each fisherman's flies

Its people are rugged, every heart is of pure gold
their souls feed from its deep beauty, each is brave and bold
They're the most blessed from all that roam this planet earth
for each Montanan well understands their land's priceless worth

For far below the stars, from God's given hand
lies my home, a place called Montana Land
A land of boundless beauty and ice-cold descending streams
Cowboys and horses and remembered Indian dreams

THE VOICE OF THE WESTERN WIND

Have you ever heard The Voice Of The Western Wind
whisper to your heart as it softly blew by?
Have you ever watched one of its beautiful painted sunsets
vanish into its ever-changing, forever-blue sky?

Have you ever felt one of its many rainbows touch your heart
after a renewing summer's rain had washed its lands anew?
Have you ever shared its deep, haunting beauty with another
while bathed in the light of a lover's moon shining for two?

Have you ever wondered about the magic spells it casts
upon each soul, that happens to travel its way?
Have you ever seen that knowing and peaceful look
deep within the eyes of those who have come and stayed?

Have you ever felt the hardness of its long winters of white
that births more stars than our summer dreams can see?
Have you ever taken a drink from one of its pure mountain streams
that's known to send a heart soaring toward Heaven forever free?

Have you ever wondered just who made its vast lands
that causes both the poet and painter to feed our human dreams?
Have you ever listened to its quiet, early morning stillness
and then have it broken by the cries of wild eagle screams?

Have you ever tasted the freshness of its fall breath
mixed with the scent of pine and sage brush in bloom?
Have you ever listened to the lingering late summer call
of a young coyote howling at the rising of its first full moon?

Have you ever felt the beating pulse of its first born
who once ruled all its lands with understanding and pride?
Have you ever traveled on one of its many liquid ice rivers
allowing its spirit to be your friend and water guide?

So, have you ever heard The Voice Of The Western Wind
whisper deep into your heart as it softly blew by?
Have you ever watched one of its beautiful sunsets
vanish into its ever changing, forever-blue sky?

SCRAPBOOK MEMORIES

It seems like it was just yesterday
that I was young and strong
But now my bathroom mirror daily reminds me
that my youth and strength are gone

But that's okay for I've been so deeply blessed
with each of my many given years
They've all brought me a lifetime of true richness
For my scrapbook is overflowing with joys and some shed tears

First memories of a mom and dad who really loved me
My early Christmases with tons of Santa's little boy toys
Great birthday parties with lots of cake and rich ice cream
and everything else that filled me with wonderment and joy

Small pieces of memories of my dad fighting in World War II
Those air raid drills, black curtains and my then fearful tears
Special memories of those fun-filled kid summers of the 1940s
Those games we played in our back alleys without crime or fear

Scrapbook Memories of all my years I spent going to school
learning the things my teachers wanted me to know
My endless lost hours daydreaming out the school windows
praying that God would soon send lots of school closing snow

Memories of my very first kiss with a girl—my first date
My first driver's license and being able to stay out late
My fun years of drag racing fast cars and drinking beer
My heart's hard lessons of puppy love from my teenage years

My sad memories of losing good friends and family
along our ever-dangerous road of life
Finally finding the girl of my dreams
and asking her to be my mate, my wife

Memories of our lasting and Christian marriage
Our two sons and a daughter, each born with their mother's eyes
Our still growing army of happy and healthy grandchildren
Our taken chance to raise them all under Montana's blue skies

Memories of father-son then son-father hunting and fishing trips
My late God-given gift of writing about Montana where we live
Memories of all the spent years of watching the world go by
Finally learning what it really means to love and give

Memories of our long years spent raising six foster children
and all of their many joys and sometimes deep pain
Watching them all grow up too quickly
and seeing their coming time of their own memories to gain

For it seems like it was just yesterday
that I was so young and so strong
But now my truthful bathroom mirror daily reminds me
that my youth and remembered strength are now gone

But that's really okay for I've been so deeply blessed
with each of my many given years
For each one has brought me a lifetime of true richness
For my life's scrapbook is overflowing now with many joys
and so many of my own personal shed tears

THE COWBOY WAY

Now there are many ways to live a life
You can stay single or find a helpmate wife
You can live in a great city or a very small town
You can run a great company or work as a clown

Now I've found what's really the best way for me
I've found the perfect job to stay happy and free
And since I found it, I plan to never change or ever stray
I've found my piece of Heaven by doing it The Cowboy Way

For it has put me in the great western outdoors
I'll never be money-rich, but then I'll never be money-poor
I'm always branding cattle and doing lots of fun cowboy things
I've even learned how to play the guitar and cowboy sing

So, there are many ways to live your life
You can stay single or find a helpmate wife
You can live in a great city or a very small town
You can even run a great company or work as a clown

But I've found what's really the best way for me
I've found the perfect job to stay happy and free
And since I found it, I plan to never change or ever stray
For I've found my piece of Heaven by doing it The Cowboy Way

Made in the USA
Lexington, KY
11 July 2019